CW00951996

# THE GETAWAYS

Vans and Life
in the Great Outdoors

gestalten

# Choosing Life on the Road

*The promise of an ever-changing everyday life has people all over the world taking to the road, downsizing their lives into vans for expansive days ahead.*

What if you could pull back the curtain of morning to a new view each day? Call the foot of the Jura Mountains your temporary office? Venture off-road into the sweeping sand dunes of the Sahara for a few days of total peace? Dip into the Mediterranean any day of the week? Or take a hike on the Andes High Plateau, and return to the comfort of your compact roving home at the end of the day?

Every day on the road is an adventure, and never has it been more possible to seek it out for yourself.

Vanlife is the search for a more experiential life outside of dense city centers. It offers an escape from a static life of commutes, work hours that far exceed the nine-to-five, and a few weeks a year to unwind if you're lucky. It is a downscaled, but high-potential lifestyle that has emerged in response to skyrocketing housing prices in our modern cities and the prohibitive cost of living. These shortcomings of contemporary life have been especially laid bare in the wake of the Covid-19 pandemic, with swathes of people leaving the city quite literally in search of fresh air. Vanlife provides the chance to unlearn the fleeting joys of consumerism in favor of lasting connection: with nature, others, and ourselves.

Life led on the road, ironically, is about slowing your speed and tuning into the minutiae of the world around you—for this is where the adventure lies.

In *Vanlife Diaries,* Kathleen Morton captures the sentiment of many who choose this itinerant life: "This community is seeking out alternatives to the debt-work-consume cycle that rules life in the new millennium. We live out of vehicles to have time to chase our passions. We choose to live on less... Out on our own terms, we're discovering a better, saner way to live."

The roots of roving life run deep. Although we have roamed and transported goods for time immemorial, it wasn't until the postwar period that recreational motor homes were available to the masses. In 1950, Volkswagen (VW) released its first bus, the enduring Type 2. Its boxy design was built to transport goods in postwar Europe, but in it, humans saw greater potential. VW went on to work with Westfalia to create the iconic van we know today, outfitting it with everyday luxuries for the road that transformed an itinerant vehicle into a comfortable home. The model ticked various boxes: it was affordable, comfortable, durable, and, perhaps most importantly to the movement it continues to inspire today, adaptable. It beckoned a free lifestyle and sowed

the seeds for a soul-searching movement. As Mike Harding writes in *The VW Camper Van,* the VW "... has taken millions of people on voyages of discovery where they often discover more about what is going on inside their souls than in the outside world."

The vanlife movement truly took off in the 1960s, fed by the youth counterculture movement. Writing for *The Weekender* in *The Daily Californian,* Jacqueline Moran notes: "Vans became a communal form of escapism, where nomads could band together and live beyond the broken conventions of 1970s society. Van culture became a kinetic network, connecting people who shared visions of an alternative lifestyle." Today, this sentiment lives on.

In its exaltation of simplicity, the vanlife movement is kindred with the tiny house movement. Both have been brewing in tandem since the '70s, veering away from the materialism of our consumerist society in favor of an achievable, arcadian life, lived inside a comfortably compact and sustainable home. In many ways, van conversions draw from the spatial innovations of the tiny house movement, outfitting vans with the efficiency of a pocketknife to include everything from fully equipped kitchens, bathrooms and toilets, outdoor terraces, ingenious storage, and living areas with all the comforting flair of a stationary home.

In tune with the desire to live a more considered life with a deeper connection to nature, a vast majority of van conversions prioritize sustainable means of living off-grid. These days, for example, vehicles can be fitted with power-generating solar panels and water filtration systems that render any source of water drinkable, making them highly self-sufficient. And it has never been easier to maintain this flexible lifestyle in the long term. With only a Wi-Fi signal, the "digital nomad" can work from anywhere, escaping commutes and dense urban centers, with the space to decompress from burnout culture and our productivity-focused lifestyles. Combined with ever-reliable four-wheel drive and high ground clearance, vans are well equipped to travel off-road to destinations far off the beaten track, allowing for an immersive, slow travel experience that contrasts with an environmentally taxing, jet-setting lifestyle. Traveling by van means traveling more slowly, connecting with locals and fellow travelers by happenstance, watching the landscape change outside your window before parking up and heading out to explore on foot.

Australian photographer and vanlifer Lauren Sutton, who is featured in this book, best sums this up: "Often when we travel, we move from one must-see location to the next, but we miss the in between. The journey is what makes seeing these locations so special. On the road you see every sunrise, every sunset, you experience the sunshine, the heat, the rain, the snow, and the cold."

The concept of vanlife, by now, has proliferated globally, notably in the form of an Instagram hashtag. It would, however, be a disservice to reduce it to an aesthetic movement, for, like many things on social media, it shows only a partial, idealized version. In an *Insider*-published piece, Canadian vanlifer Matt Watson sagely noted, "When you're scrolling through the hashtag and seeing the back doors open on a beach, it's dreamlike. It's not real. If you go in expecting that, you're going to miss out on the beauty of the journey that you're actually on." Instead, he contends, vanlife culture is about having "no expectations," and "leaving" yourself open to find joy in simplicity."

And in this simplicity, the benefits for well-being are manifold. The experience of vanlife forces one to be in the present. Nature, with all its awe-inspiring beauty and spirit-testing whims, is right at your doorstep, every day. The advantage of being outdoors is self-evident— just think of the restorative quality of a walk to ease the mind—but it is also being corroborated by research. In 2020, the Yale School of the Environment published an article detailing various scientific studies that showed the positive effects of time spent in nature—on everything from our stress levels and sense of connectedness to our immune system and blood pressure. "Nature is not only nice to have, but it's a have-to-have for physical health and cognitive functioning," says journalist Richard Louv. Then there is the life-affirming power of lived experience. Research shows that the happiness payoff we get from spending on an experience is far greater and far longer lasting than any material possession we could buy. Experiences provide for us long after we've lived through them, becoming anecdotes we reflect on, connect with, and share. When you live on the road, your cup of experience is brimful every day, to the point of running over. ■

# Camper-Vanning in a Cold Climate

*From key safety gear to crafting cozy interiors, here's
a starter pack for all your cool-weather needs*

### 1. Navigation Software

Traveling in cooler climates requires planning—ice,
snow, and sleet can make for dangerous and difficult driving.
Download GPS navigation software to your phone in
advance, and check weather warnings along your route
to avoid hazardous conditions.

### 3. Snow Tires and Chains

Keep tire chains on hand for cold-weather adventures.
When there's snow, ice, or mud on the road, these exterior
chains create the necessary traction to keep your vehicle
moving. However, prolonged chain use can damage tires,
so rely on good snow tires for longer journeys.

### 2. Ice Scraper

When it comes to clearing ice and snow from your
windows, an efficient ice scraper is key. If you're headed
out on a particularly frosty trip, it's worth splurging.
Swedish scrapers are famously well made, while those
with extendable handles are easier to operate.

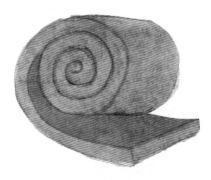

### 4. Insulation

Proper insulation is vital when it comes to winter-proofing
your van. Spray foam is widely hailed as the most effective
insulator, but other options include sheep's wool and
Polyiso foam board. Insulated window covers complete
the package for a truly toasty night's sleep.

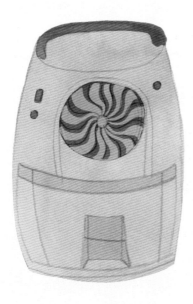

## 5. Dehumidifier

A dehumidifier helps prevent condensation and excess moisture from amassing inside your van, and stops mildew and mold in their tracks. It also reduces the feeling of perceived cold, which is at its most intense in chilly, humid climates.

## 7. Heater

Of course, you also need van-suitable heating to generate warmth. Diesel and gasoline heaters are the most energy-efficient options, while propane furnaces and electric or wood-burning stoves are also common choices (the latter requiring an axe and a competent chopper).

## 8. Doormat

A doormat in rubber or coir will not only limit the amount of muck and dirt you track into your van come wintertime, but can also double as a nifty traction mat should you find your tires stuck and endlessly spinning on icy or muddy ground.

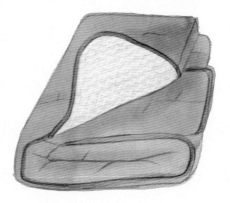

## 6. Safety Equipment

Before you go, make a safety-gear checklist and restock your tool and first-aid kits. Tow straps, a portable jump starter, road flares, and a high-vis vest are essential—as are a winch and spare tire. Gloves, emergency blankets, and a snow shovel are your winter go-tos.

## 9. Warm Bedding

A comfortable bed is a vanlifer's best friend in any climate, but winter-proofing your sleeping area can make all the difference on a long, cold road trip. A feather duvet or thick down sleeping bag, plus a stash of fleece or wool blankets, is advisable.

# Quintessentials for Temperate Conditions

*Stabilizers, speakers, and solar panels: basics for living your best vanlife, whatever the weather*

### 1. Leveling Equipment

Unless you're parked on flat ground, you're going to need leveling gear to keep your van level. Use blocks, ramps, jack pads, and chocks to stop the wheels from moving while you level up. Installing a permanent level indicator will speed up the process.

### 3. Toilet

A good van toilet should make your life simpler, not stinkier. The best models span compost toilets that combine solid waste with compostable peat, chemical porta-potties (which can also be used with eco-friendly alternatives), and installable, large-tank latriness.

### 2. Solar Panels

Incorporating solar panels into your van's electrical design is a no-brainer. By harnessing the sun's power, you can reduce your dependence on fuel-guzzling generators and electric hookups, give back to both the environment and your wallet, and camp out in the wild for longer.

### 4. Cargo Box

In vanlife, a little extra space goes a long way, which is why external cargo boxes are such a smart storage solution. You can opt for a rooftop box, a soft, waterproof cargo bag, or a tailer-hitch cargo carrier (which requires a tailer-hitch receiver, too).

### 5. Car Charger

A 12-volt inverter is invaluable for charging on the go. Replete with multiple sockets, catering to USB, DC, and 110V AC-powered devices alike, this charger allows you to pull power from your vehicle's battery to get your gadgets back up and running in no time at all.

### 7. Wi-Fi Range Extender

Securing a sufficient internet connection on the road is an irksome but often imperative task. Happily, a Wi-Fi range extender can boost your internet's reliability and speed, while cellular boosters are similarly handy for remote areas with poor reception.

### 8. Portable Speaker

While some may consider it superfluous, a portable Bluetooth speaker is a van-life enhancer that shouldn't be overlooked. Opt for a lightweight, waterproof model with a long battery life—even better if it has the capacity to charge other USB-powered devices too.

### 6. Fire Extinguisher

It's extremely important to implement fire-safety measures inside your van. Purchase a multipurpose fire extinguisher that can counteract liquid, gas, and electrical fires. Replace it every five years, and make sure to mount a fire blanket and install smoke alarm, too.

### 9. Headlamp

Whether you need both hands for nighttime repairs or want to grab another drink from the fridge without waking your fellow campers, you'll be surprised how quickly a headlamp makes itself indispensable. You can also use it as a signaling device in case of breakdowns.

# Warm-Weather Necessities for Off-Grid Adventuring

*Tools for keeping calm, cool, and critter-free in the heat,
so you can make the most of your surroundings*

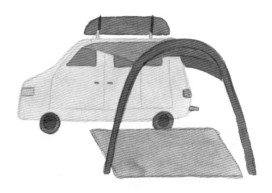

### 1. Citronella Candles

If you want to further deter marauding mosquitoes, giant citronella candles can also help keep bugs at bay—plus, they look and smell lovely. You can buy them or make your own from citronella oil and beeswax. Just be sure to follow fire-safety guidelines.

### 3. Awning

Awnings are a hot-weather, off-grid essential. They markedly expand your living space, while providing much-needed shelter from sunshine and summer downpours alike. The best models attach to the sides or roof of your vehicle for easy assembly and space efficiency.

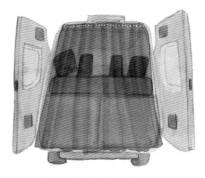

### 2. Ceiling Fan

A vent fan is an ideal way to circulate cool, fresh air around your van, and is particularly useful in instances when leaving your windows open isn't an option. Affordable and easy to install, most models are remote-control operated and offer multiple speed settings.

### 4. Bug Screens

There are few things more disruptive to a good night's sleep than insect invaders, especially mosquitoes. When the heat is too stifling to shutter up, a good set of bug screens—ideally ones designed for your specific camper, to ensure a secure fit—is a key investment.

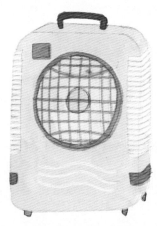

**5. Portable AC**

For extra warm or humid climates, a portable air conditioner may be necessary to regulate your van's temperature and air quality. Many also have built-in dehumidifiers. Remember to check the AC's BTU rating (i.e., cooling capacity) to make sure it's the right size for your van.

**6. Fridge**

With a 12-volt refrigerator, you can venture well off the beaten track while keeping your food fresh and drinks cold. Seek out top-loading units designed for vans to maximize space (both internally and externally). These often come with a freezer section too.

**7. Outdoor Kitchenette**

If you're a mostly warm-weather camper, consider integrating a pull-out kitchenette into your van design. Usually equipped with a sink, cooktop, and extra counter space, galley kitchens can vastly expand your cooking area, enabling you to whip up feasts under the stars.

**8. Outdoor Shower**

Likewise, an outdoor shower is a great space-maker (and money saver) for summertime travelers. Options abound, from tankless, propane, or electricity-fueled models to roof-mounted, fresh-water showers with built-in solar panels. Don't forget your biodegradable soap!

**9. Outdoor Furniture**

Outdoor furniture helps you make the most of your new surroundings. There are all sorts of fold-up and pull-out tables and chairs available, so do your research: make sure they're comfortable, compact, and durable. And invest in a hammock for afternoon siestas.

# A Birch-Decked Bus for Adventures Near and Far

Partners Alena Reinecke and Jonathan Steinhoff had always dreamed of traveling the world after graduating from college, but when that time arrived, they changed tack, opting to redirect their focus a little closer to home. "We thought, 'There are so many beautiful places in and around Germany, our home country, why not explore Europe first?' And what better way to do it than by bus?" the couple explains. "Steinhoff had grown up with Volkswagen T3 vans, and always loved old buses and the idea of traveling with them, so we quickly came to the conclusion that that was what we wanted."

They were delighted to find a partially deconstructed, seven-seater Volkswagen T2b bus ("That's even cooler than a T3, isn't it?") and soon set themselves the task of getting the vehicle restored, converted, and back on the road—with a little help from Steinhoff's van-savvy father. "We liked the original look of the bus, which we named Sepp. We had fallen in love with its beige and green color scheme, a rather rare combination that was only sold on the U.S. market in 1979, so we changed the exterior as little as possible," they say of the renovation process.

When it came to Sepp's interior, however, they had their work cut out for them. "We liked the original Westfalia build-outs, but not so much the materials that were used back then," the duo expands, "so we replicated the style but built it out of birch multiplex boards instead." They outsourced the creation of the CNC-milled birch headliner to a local carpentry business but designed and crafted the rest of the space entirely by themselves, from the sculpturally rendered, roughly sanded cabinets, shelves, and countertop to the classic Westfalia-style bench-to-bed system and custom kitchen tap, which they constructed from an old copper heating pipe.

For the upholstery, they selected a complementary olive, beige, and black-checkered pattern in homage to the original Volkswagen plaid, and green curtains to match the exterior. These elements, paired with the warm, honey-colored wood and the soft glow of the van's rear string lights, conjure up a delightfully welcoming space that is as chic as it is cozy.

Reinecke and Steinhoff have traveled around 26,000 kilometers (16,000 miles) in Sepp to date, journeying across Germany, Switzerland, Austria, France, Denmark, Finland, Norway, Sweden, and the Faroe

*Adventuring along northern coastlines (opposite).*

Islands. "The flair and feel of driving and traveling with the bus is hard to put into words," they enthuse. "It's always an adventure!"

Their favorite experience so far is a recent three-month trip they took through Scandinavia, right up to the Nordkapp, (enviable snapshots from which adorn their expertly curated Instagram feed). "After three months, more than 9,000 kilometers (5,600 miles), and so many beautiful places, we safely returned back home to northern Germany," Steinhoff recounts. But while Sepp's engine held out for the duration of the trip, the pair are now in the process of having to rebuild it. "That's been the biggest challenge we've faced so far, but we guess you sign up for the task when you buy an old bus like Sepp," they concede. ■

## DETAILED VEHICLE INFORMATION

Sepp is a second-generation model of the Volkswagen Type 2—a T2b or "Late Bay" to be precise, the term for versions of the bus made after 1972. Particularly coveted today for their singularly charming aesthetic, these precursors to modern cargo and passenger vans remain a firm off-grid favorite. Sepp's colorway is unusual in Germany, but not as unusual as its tasteful interior, crafted by hand from birch in an exceptionally refined take on the Westfalia-style layout.

| Manufacturer | VOLKSWAGEN | Year | 1979 |
|---|---|---|---|
| Model | T2B | Mileage | UNKNOWN |

Sunrise over the sea (*above*).
A modern take, in birch,
on Westfalia's bench-to-bed
system (*opposite*).

# An Otherworldly Road Trip Along Iceland's Ring Road

*In a small-but-mighty Nissan, Daniel Müller and Elena Strütt break from their urban life to follow Iceland's mythical Ring Road.*

**Iceland** | Photographer Daniel Müller and his wife, florist Elena Strütt, spent June 2016 on an unforgettable road trip along Iceland's 1,328-kilometer-long (825-mile-long) Ring Road. "Both my wife and I were very keen to get out of the bustling concrete jungle of Berlin for a while," explains Müller. With its rugged volcanic landscape filled with otherworldly sights, Iceland promised just that. And though it may not have been the obvious summer adventure—in June, temperatures reach an average high of 12.8 °C (55 °F) and drop to lows of 5.4 °C (42 °F)—it's by far the best time of year to explore Iceland on four wheels, with long daylight hours allowing one to make the most of the dramatic landscape.

Müller and Strütt hit the road in a compact, converted Nissan NV200, kitted out with the basics: a sleeping area in the rear cabin, a cooler, folding chairs, a collapsible table, and plenty of storage space for cooking utensils. The indoor-outdoor model at times proved trying: "Icelandic weather can be quite rough and uncomfortable," says Müller. "Sometimes it was a challenge to prepare dinner after a long day on the road. We didn't have a spacious van to prepare meals inside so we had to create some makeshift wind stoppers so our gas stove wouldn't be blown out." It wasn't, however, a deal breaker, and in the end, the simplicity of their vehicle won out. "Of course," he reflects, "you could always go for a bigger van with a little kitchen nook inside, or where you'd be able to stand. But do you actually need it? At times it was challenging … but hopping inside the warm van afterwards and having a meal was quite rewarding."

Their route started counterclockwise, just east of Reykjavík, following the 300-kilometer (186-mile) Golden Circle route, where many first see Iceland's natural wonders: from the Þingvellir National Park, which straddles a rift valley between North American and Eurasian tectonic plates, to Kerið, a 3,000-year-old volcanic crater lake.

From here, the pair headed east along the south coast. The road here is lined with waterfalls, so commonplace in Iceland and yet unfailingly wondrous. Müller recommends stepping out to see Seljalandsfoss up close: an opening in the cliff face means visitors are afforded the unique opportunity of stepping behind the cascading water. Their first overnight stop was the small township of Vík í Mýrdal, famous for its volcanic, black-sand beaches with unparalleled views: Dyrhólaey with its natural arched rock face, formed by flowing lava, and Reynisdrangar with its stepped basalt rock formation, nicknamed "Troll's toes," where puffins roost.

But in Iceland, there is always something more. "It's hard to say which of the many sights would be my highlight, as there are nonstop highlights along the way. I guess the fact that the landscape changed drastically within minutes was quite astonishing and fascinating," says Müller.

From Vík í Mýrdal, they visited the pillowy soft moss-covered lava field Eldhraun, created by an eruption in 1783, then ventured into the frozen interior, stopping for a guided hike on one of the glacier tongues of Hvannadalshnúkur at Skaftafell National Park. The national park sits at the foot of the vast Vatnajökull Glacier, which makes up a huge 8 percent of Iceland's landmass. Close by, the magical glacier lagoon Jökulsárlón tints everything a soft ice blue.

Continuing along the island's far east, they began to wind along their first fjords, before the Ring Road veered inland, leading them up to Egilsstaðir, at the bank of the Lagarfljót River, to set up camp. Just north of the town, the road turns left sharply, bypassing Iceland's remote northeast corner. The true north holds many wonders, including moody Dettifoss, a thunderous waterfall that is Europe's second most powerful, and Hverarönd, an arid geothermal

The black volcanic sands of Vík í Mýrdal, Iceland *(opposite).*

Icelandic horses in their
element *(above)*. A natural
rock bridge in Arnarstapi
*(right)*. A quiet stretch on
the Ring Road *(opposite)*.

landscape that is distinguishably alive underfoot:
sulfuric steam rises from fumaroles and boiling
mud pots bubble energetically.

    In the island's northwest, they stopped at
the basalt dragon-like rock formation Hvítserkur
before continuing to the southwest, stopping south
of the Snæfellsnes Peninsula to stay in the fishing
village Arnarstapi before returning to the capital.
The journey proved a formative first trip for the couple,
now married and parents to a one-year-old. "This
was our first vacation together," says Müller, "and you
can imagine that spending a few days together
on the road can help you to either bond or disagree
on a lot of things. Luckily, we enjoyed each other's
company and the scenic route very much." ∎

ICELAND

Reykjavík

Arnarstapi

Hvítserkur

Þingvellir
National Park

Keríð

Seljalandsfoss

Vík í Mýrdal

Eldhraun

Hvannadalshnúkur

Jökulsárlón

Hverarönd

Dettifoss

Egilsstaðir

Skirting volcanic mountainscapes *(opposite)*. The Seljavallalaug swimming pool *(top)*. One of Iceland's many waterfalls *(bottom left)*. Strütt in a field of lupines *(bottom right)*.

# Always North, Always Norway

*Ever enchanted by Norway, nature photographers Natascha Klein and Daniel Ernst returned for a gas-guzzling trip that left no road less taken.*

**Norway** | "To me, Norway means vastness, silence, and endless beautiful nature. In no country do I feel so free, and that is the reason why I travel there again and again," says dedicated vanlifer Natascha Klein. A landscape and travel photographer, she hits the road in a 20-year-old converted Volkswagen T5 Transporter, "Wilma," with her husband and co-photographer Daniel Ernst. They've traveled far and wide across mainland Europe and the Nordic countries, but it's Norway they keep coming back to, choosing to heading there in summer when vast swathes of Europeans head south. "My route has mostly been through the southern fjords of Norway to Helgeland, where there are beautiful islands with Caribbean-like beaches in the middle of the ocean, then over the Atlantic Ocean Road, through countless national parks to the Lofoten Islands, and the island of Senja," explains Klein. "From there, as in 2020, we went up to Nordkapp and along Finnmark to the easternmost point of Norway, which is further east than Istanbul and Cairo." Despite the breathtaking beaches, the climate is anything but Caribbean, and summer in Norway is often best enjoyed with a layer of down. Vardø, on the far eastern front, looks out over the Barent Sea, and peak summer temperatures reach an average height of only 12°C (54°F). Essential for their

Norwegian travel is their van's diesel heater. "I always feel cold, and the heater is like a hero in such moments," says Klein.

Nonetheless, their third trip, in the summer of 2020, was their best yet. As soon as Norway reopened its borders, they decided to head back up to the northeast, taking on an over 10,000-kilometer (6,214-mile) journey to expand on their previous travels. "The trip in 2020 was probably so special because we drove through the whole country within four weeks," shares Klein. Out their window, the landscape shifted dramatically the further they went. "To see how diverse the country is, how the landscape changes from region to region, and also the people who live there, that was just fascinating… I will definitely never forget this trip." They were in good company, too, traveling alongside close friends in a matching Volkswagen T5 Transporter; they stopped for hiking trips in Rago National Park, with its impressive terrain of waterfalls, mountains, forests, and cliffs.

Together, they continued on the road, heading to the picturesque archipelago of Lofoten. There, they encountered the full mood of Norwegian "summer," as they hiked through a brutal storm to a remote cabin. Undeterred after drying off, they planned a 490-meter (1,607-foot) ascent of Tindstinden peak. Its breathtaking views were only rivaled by those seen during their unique experience chartering a small aircraft, where they took in the aerial views of the archipelago's dramatic, cloud-skirting peaks and the dark, glassy sea that engulfs them.

Despite all the ground covered, the couple's Norwegian travels usually start without a precise plan. "I am so in love with this country that my biggest goal is always to spend as much time as possible here and to get to know as many places and regions as possible," shares Klein. "By traveling slowly in the van, you get the chance to really get to know a country: the nature, the people, the culture. We rarely set specific places as a goal—the main thing is to just enjoy the time in the place we love the most and not stress ourselves." One thing that does continually guide them is a shared desire to capture the landscape on camera. "My husband and I are both landscape and travel photographers, and, therefore, deal a lot with photogenic places that we would like to travel to and photograph. We watch a lot of documentaries, talk to friends who live there, and, of course, often get inspired via social media. In this way, more and more places appear on our map, which we mark and travel to," says Klein.

A small seaside town, Norway *(opposite)*.

Setting up camp on the beach
*(opposite, bottom right)*.
Strolling along the Lofoten
Islands *(opposite, bottom left)*.
The kitchen, illuminated by
skylight *(left)*. A reindeer
crossing *(above)*.

On their 2020 trip, just two hours north of
Tromsø, Wilma's shaft broke. They found themselves
stuck in a 6-kilometer (3.7-mile) tunnel and after a
six-hour wait to be towed, found that Wilma had to be
shipped home, as no local workshop could tackle
the issue. Not wanting to cut their trip to Nordkapp short,
they finished off their adventure in a rented Volvo
with a much-too-small trunk. "We did not let the mood
be spoiled, and packed only the most important
things in a bag, rented a car, and slept in it for a week. You
know, when you feel like nothing more can go wrong,
sometimes you have the best and most fun time ever!" ∎

# NORWAY

Nordkapp

Varangerhalvøya National Park

Tromsø

RUSSIA

Tindstinden, Lofoten

Rago National Park

SWEDEN

FINLAND

A puppy pause *(bottom left)*.
A convoy with a dramatic view
*(bottom right)*. Looking out
at the mountains *(opposite)*.

# A Cabin-Like Camper to Aid Creativity

When British couple Amy Spires and Steven Mackus found themselves stuck at home during the first Covid-19 lockdown, both suspectedly sick with the virus, they came to the realization that the life they had been living wasn't making them happy. Shortly after, they quit their jobs, sold their house, and headed for Scotland in their small, converted van to discover a new life on the road.

Once there, they quickly fell in love with vanlife and the myriad opportunities it gifted them: freed from expensive living costs, Spires had taken up weaving, while Mackus embraced wood carving, and they had never been more content. All they needed now was a bigger camper. "We didn't want to take time out to convert another van from scratch," explains Spires, "so we decided to find an old motor home with character and a good base interior to lend our personal touch to." They settled upon a 1989 Talbot Express Pilote R470, which they found on Facebook Marketplace. "We loved the original '80s motor home interior," says Mackus of their choice. "The wood paneling, the orangey-brown sink and cooker. We decided to keep as much of it as possible but to give it more of a 'cabin' feel."

"We wanted it to be a smaller version of the home we'd sold: bright and airy with touches of reclaimed wood and antique pieces," chimes in Spires, explaining that they achieved this by "painting the walls a lighter color, keeping the wooden cupboards, and building new wood tabletops from vintage furniture." They also removed some of the original furnishings to create more floor space and to make room for a sofa and a covetable wood-burning stove made by Anevay Stoves in Cornwall—a necessity in Scotland's famously chilly climate.

The result is a homey yet picturesque space that, importantly, doubles as a place for the couple to craft their handmade products, which they sell on Etsy. "The van is designed to be a traveling workshop and studio," says Spires. "We've added a large workbench at the back where we can work on pieces for our shop and wrap and photograph orders," expands Mackus. Spires's favorite element of their tiny home is the windows, which she says are vital to the creation process. "Every single side of the van has at least one window, which means we get light no matter where or what angle

The Talbot weathering the Scottish climate (opposite).

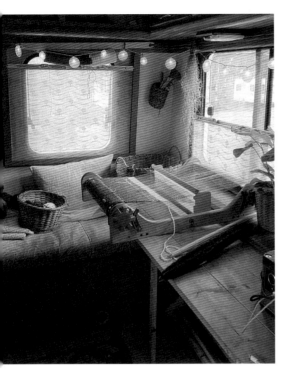

The loom station *(above left)*. Beginnings of crafts to be sold online *(above right)*. The cozy fireside nook *(right)*.

we're parked at, which is perfect when you're working." Mackus, meanwhile, most enjoys the van's age and history. "A lot of older people approach us and tell us about the Talbots they used to own, and how much joy they brought them," he enthuses.

Spires and Mackus have put their Talbot to the test on many a Scottish foray. "One of the worst experiences was on the Isle of Skye, where the wind became so bad one night that the doors were rattling, and the van was rocking. We thought we were going to blow away!" the couple recalls. Yet, they also had one of their most rewarding van experiences on the very same island. "We managed to get up an incredibly perilous, narrow road that took us to a lovely remote beach," says Mackus. "The road was so steep that our front wheels were skidding around, and I genuinely didn't think we'd make it at one point. A lot of people think you're limited as to where you can go in a big old motor home, but it's never failed us, even if it means going very, very slowly," he says. "Plus, you can't beat the amount of freedom it brings," concludes Spires of the duo's improved way of life, all thanks to their trusty Talbot. ∎

## DETAILED VEHICLE INFORMATION

The Talbot Express, which came in a variety of sturdy vans, was the last Talbot vehicle ever produced and was sold exclusively in the U.K. It proved a popular choice of motor home thanks to its size and relatively energy-efficient diesel engine, given its considerable weight. Spires and Mackus chose their 1989 van for its "character" and charming, mostly wooden base interior. This, they say, made it simpler to adapt to their taste, addeding touches like a large workbench and cozy wood-burning stove.

| Manufacturer | TALBOT | Year | 1989 |
|---|---|---|---|
| Model | EXPRESS PILOTE R470 | Mileage | 129,000 KM (80,000 MI) |

A pause out on the moors (*above*).

# A Snowboarding Adventure to Hokkaido's Core

*Friends, filmmakers, and snowboarders Henry Johnson and Charlie Wood trucked through Hokkaido in search of the best powder.*

**Japan** | Anyone witnessing Henry Johnson and Charlie Wood's delightfully quirky truck "Sabi-chan" might find themselves wondering: Is it a truck? Is it a cabin? Or a tiny home? The answer is all of those, and more. Constructed from upcycled materials and built atop a Honda Acty Kei Truck, a popular Japanese mini pickup, the vehicle took handyman Johnson and filmmaker Wood, both avid snowboarders, through Hokkaido, Japan's northernmost island, in early 2020 to make their short film *Wabi Sabi: An Adventure in Northern Japan.* "We decided it would be a fun project to document together and get out and explore more of Hokkaido's interior. The main goal was to ride the famous Hokkaido powder the area is renowned for, meeting friends new and old along the way."

Johnson used upcycled, salvaged materials, many of them sourced from friends, including the pitched, corrugated-iron roof on top and the various materials used to create its striking collage of shingles on the exterior. "It had been a dream of mine for a while to create the small camper on the back of a Kei truck," explains Johnson. "Sabi-chan is a great home on the road. It serves its job well as a home base for backcountry riding. It is just big enough for two to sleep relatively comfortably and have ample storage space for gear," he continues. Traveling during Japan's frosty winter, however, did pose challenges. "The main concern was the lack of heating. This meant that evenings were cold, sleeping in full clothing and puffer jackets wrapped in a sleeping bag, but still feeling the cold biting at your extremities. This meant that once the morning came around, the glow and warmth of the sun coming through the side window was that much more appreciated!" On the plus side, wherever they found themselves along the way, they were never short of conversation: "Traveling in Sabi-chan always came with its perks, like driving past the smiling faces of slightly confused locals at the sight of the camper," says Johnson. "People would stop by when we were parked up to come and have a look for themselves. Everyone was so positive and happy to see it!"

The duo started off at home in Kimobetsu, southwest of Sapporo, before stopping at Niseko Tokyu Grand Hirafu ski resort at the foot of the volcano Mount Yōtei. From there, they stocked up on gas-station Onigiri (rice balls) and riding snacks and headed to their approximate destination—east—to let the journey unfold.

Their first major stop was Daisetsuzan National Park, located in Hokkaido's mountainous interior. "As we left town on day one, we were delighted to check the forecast for the days that would follow, and there was a big storm on the way, delivering the much-anticipated, white-gold powder we love to ride on," explains Johnson. "This arrived overnight, and we had a very hectic drive in very deep snow—exhilarating to say the least! The camper held up in these conditions, and we were on the edge of our seats until we reached our destination!"

But out on the slopes, on just day three, Wood dislocated his shoulder while snowboarding and had to be raced to Asahikawa for medical attention. Afterwards, he was determined to keep going and adjusted his style of filming. "Following this," explains Johnson, "I could now ride roadside spots, or anywhere that he could film via a long lens as riding for him was now off the cards." They decided to leave the slopes and instead headed further east to take in the sights. They found a standout view at the northern Sea of Okhotsk: "Cape Notoro, where drift sea ice is abundant, and as far as the eye can see, there are large blocks of ice floating out to the horizon." From there, they continued along the coast to Shari, driving to the southern town of Kushiro on the North Pacific Coast, and eventually looping back to Sapporo.

Volcanic ocean views from Hokkaido, Japan *(opposite).*

The small-but-mighty Kei truck traverses the snow *(above)*. Catching reflections *(right)*. A friend rides up front *(opposite, bottom left)*. The snowboarding station *(opposite, bottom right)*.

In the end, their film was made, capturing the highs, lows, and wonders of their snowboarding adventure. "We had the ultimate feeling of freedom, even if just for a week." And no matter the challenges along the way, there was always a place to unwind in natural hot springs, known as wild onsen. "They are a huge highlight of van traveling in Japan. Being able to relax in a steaming hot pool among the snow in the wilderness is the perfect way to rest and recuperate a worn-out body," says Johnson. ∎

JAPAN

Hokkaido

Cape Notoro
Abashiri
Shari
Kamikawa
Asahikawa
Higashikawa
Furano
Kushiro
Sapporo
Nakayama
Obihiro
Chitose

Niseko
Kimobetsu

Snowboarding in Hokkaido *(opposite)*. Taking to the slopes *(top)*. Weathering a snowstorm *(bottom left)*. Sabi-chan in the neon glow *(bottom right)*.

# Once a Fire Truck, Now a Thrill Seeker

In 2015, Austrian big-mountain freerider Fabian Lentsch decided to leave the Freeride World Tour and head into the unknown, in search of skiing locations off the beaten track. He co-founded the Snowmads with producer Karin Lechner, with whom he would document the adventures on film. The team needed a reliable vehicle for difficult terrain, something that could easily be repaired in any country, and that could fit six to eight athletes and crew. The vehicle choice was inspired by Lentsch's good friend and fellow Snowmad Markus Ascher, who was already on the road in his smaller four-by-four Mercedes 310, which came complete with a woodstove. It sparked a nine-month process of researching, locating, and rebuilding a 1985 Mercedes Fire Truck. The aim was to create a perfect winter camper that could easily navigate its way through tricky-to-reach skiing terrain, in equally tricky conditions, and act as a base for the travelers. With its reliable make, four-by-four transmission that was perfect for off-roading, and ease of repair, the Mercedes ticked almost all the boxes. The challenge, however, was space. Most expedition vehicles don't tend to account for such large numbers, but by taking into account every centimeter of space available to them, they figured out a workable layout. "With eight people, it's really tight, so you'd better have no problems with being close to each other!" share the Snowmads.

The former fire truck was overhauled with a completely new cabin, measuring roughly 13 square meters (139 square feet) and sleeping a total of eight people, an alcove that sleeps up to four, a kitchen, a shower cabin (that has so far only been used to store ski equipment), and a living space that can be converted into a double bed. Thoughtful details include a dedicated cupboard for each traveler, filmmaking storage space with charging facilities, hooks above the woodstove to dry outdoor clothing, and a bunk bed that can be pushed into a cupboard when not needed, or transformed into a small work desk for editing videos. "As for the interior, we wanted to keep it as natural, cozy, and functional as possible. We used a lot of sheep's wool, untreated wood, and oak for the floor," say the Snowmads. And of course, it's fully kitted out on the outside, too, holding a ski box, among other storage boxes, and a bike rack for six mountain bikes. There's even a firewood loading zone

The striking Snowmads truck stands up to the most extreme settings (opposite).

Heading off on a skiing
adventure *(opposite)*.
Warming up by the
truck's woodstove *(above
left)*. On top of the
world *(above right)*.

that links up to the seating
area inside, for easy access.
But the favorite space
among the team is without
a doubt the roof deck,
which not only provides access to spectacular views but
is the perfect place to hang out after skiing or to hold
a yoga session.

So far, the Snowmads have made it successfully
to Austria, Germany, Slovenia, Croatia, Bosnia
and Herzegovina, Serbia, Kosovo, North Macedonia,
Albania, Greece, and Turkey. It's not been without
some hair-raising moments along steep, icy, and exposed
roads. The crew describes an incident in Turkey, when
they slid down pure ice, disguised by a layer of fresh
snow: "We were sliding backward uncontrolled ... which
ended with us sliding some hundred meters, fortunately
stopping before falling off the road." The lesson
learned? Chains need to go on early: the four-by-four
alone won't keep you from sliding. That said, this was
an exception: "Other than that, going on trips with
the Snowmads' campers, usually you're in for some
of the best, most adventurous times of your life!" ∎

## DETAILED VEHICLE INFORMATION

This former Mercedes fire truck was reworked to
accommodate a film crew, traveling athletes, and a
thirst for extreme winter sports. It now sleeps up
to eight people in its new cabin area of approximately
13 square meters (139 square feet) that houses a
kitchen, shower cabin, and living space. To support
filmmaking on the road, there are ample charging
facilities and a bunk bed that turns into a work desk.
Outside, a roof deck offers panoramic views, as
well as ample storage for equipment and a mountain
bike rack.

| Manu-facturer | MERCEDES-BENZ | Year | 1985 |
|---|---|---|---|
| Model | 1113 LAF ALLRAD | Mileage | 83,000 KM (51,574 MI) |

# Along Winding Alpine Roads

*While on the road touring Europe, Australian couple Lauren and Jack Sutton took on the heights of the Alps in their Volkswagen called Matilda.*

**The Alps** | In early May 2018, as spring began its blooming, Australian photographer Lauren Sutton and her husband Jack set off to explore northern Europe on a trip covering 35,400 kilometers (22,000 miles). Free as a roaming van, when the weather in Norway proved stormier in summer, they headed south for an alpine adventure.

The pair's vanlife beginnings stretch back to living on Tasmania, an island off the south coast of mainland Australia. It is a place of wild beauty, and to better experience it, the couple bought a van to explore new sights every weekend. Like many before them, they were inspired by the freedom that vanlife offered and began planning an extensive trip through continental Europe and the U.K. "We both ended up quitting our jobs, packed up our lives, stored them away, and headed off on the trip of a lifetime," says Lauren. "The goal was to see as much as we could and do as much as we could in the time that we had, and vanlife allowed us to do this in the best way possible."

Once they arrived in Europe, they picked up their van, a 1986 Volkswagen T3 Vanagon that had been purpose built as a self-contained camper. Now known as Matilda, she came with a built-in gas cooker and heater, plenty of storage, and a rock and roll bed. "Luckily, we didn't need to do any alterations to her

after we bought her from the previous owners. She was in pretty good condition, but being an older van, we broke down so many times!" says Lauren. "The roof leaked, the fridge didn't really work, there was no AC, and there were constant repairs to the engine. At one stage, the engine actually fell out of the van." They quickly became experts at running repairs and finding mechanics along the way. "While it would have been amazing to do the trip in a new, luxurious van, it just wouldn't have been the same trip," says Lauren.

Stretching across eight alpine countries, the Alps offer abundant van routes, especially in the more welcoming summer season, where hot days meet cool nights. "We came into Austria from Germany, then zigzagged our way across Austria, Italy, and Switzerland to France," explains Lauren. In Austria, they stopped in postcard-perfect Salzburg before venturing to the vertiginous Stüdlhütte that skirts Austria's highest mountain range, the Glockner Group. From Austria, it was into Italy and the Dolomites to the Tre Cime di Lavaredo—famed for its three battlement-like peaks and the summer hiking destinations of Cortina and Seceda—before stopping at the alpine Lake Carezza, with its deep turquoise waters and reflections of the Latemar mountains beyond. Though the weather did turn in Italy (pack all-weather clothes, recommends Lauren), after hours of idling inside the van, a treat was in store: a huge double rainbow, captured on film over Seiser Alm, a Dolomite plateau and Italy's largest high-altitude alpine meadow.

After Italy, they drove to Switzerland, first heading back up into Austria, to Innsbruck, and on to the 13th-century Ehrenberg Castle, before arriving in peaceful Appenzell. Further south, their route steepened as they braved the iconic Furka Pass. The winding ascent, with its sweeping views of glaciers, lakes, and forests, runs for 42 kilometers (26 miles) and reaches 2,431 meters (7,976 feet) above sea level, and was the site of a hair-raising car chase in the 1964 James Bond film Goldfinger. The pair finished their alpine route in the town of Zermatt, at the foot of the mesmerizing Matterhorn, one of the Alps' highest peaks.

"Other than the obvious highlights of seeing so many amazing places, I think what makes a trip like this unique is getting to experience these places from the road," shares Lauren. "Often when we travel, we move from one must-see location to the next, but we miss the in between. The journey is what makes seeing these locations so special. On the road, you see every sunrise, every sunset, you experience the sunshine, the heat, the rain, the snow, and the cold."

The stunning alpine waters of Lake Carezza, Italy *(opposite)*.

The Suttons and Matilda,
their van *(above)*. Horsing
around *(right)*. An eagle
circles a hilltop settlement
*(opposite, bottom left)*.
A remote alpine cabin
*(opposite, bottom right)*.

The mountainous routes provided wide-ranging
automotive experiences, too. "The terrain was definitely
challenging as you can expect. Matilda struggled
on the steep winding roads, we were already pretty slow
with not a lot of engine power, and we actually thought
at one stage we might not make it up one of the roads!"
But such was the bond, that the couple ended up
keeping Matilda and shipped her back to Australia,
where they plan to refurbish her and take her back
out onto the road at home. It is, Lauren says, the most
expensive souvenir they've ever bought. ■

GERMANY

Ehrenberg
Castle

Appenzell

Salzburg

AUSTRIA

LIECHTENSTEIN

THE ALPS

Innsbruck

Stüdlhütte

SWITZERLAND

Furka
Pass

Seiser Alm

Tre Crime di Lavaredo

Lake Carezza

ITALY

Zermatt

FRANCE

Exploring the peaks *(opposite)*.
A mountain chapel *(top left)*.
Alpine lakes *(top right)*.
A bloom with a view *(bottom left)*. The cozy bedroom at
dusk *(bottom right)*.

# To Awake Each Day with a New View

André Weigelt and Laura Krüger were not initially in search of vanlife. The couple was motivated, rather, by the desire to leave big-city life in Berlin behind. "It wasn't that we were explicitly looking for vans, we just stumbled across this one and bought it right away, without even doing a test-drive," they share. Their model of choice was a sandy-colored 1986 Mercedes-Benz 407 D Van, now affectionately called "Oskar the Explorer." "We love the exterior look of our van a lot—it is just so charming," they recall. From that moment on, they knew that the van wasn't just going to be for a weekend getaway. The pair wanted to travel long-term and leave the city for good.

With this intention in mind, the number one priority of the rebuild was livability. "It had to be comfortable for two people to live in it. We wanted a kitchen so we could cook real meals and enough space to also spend bad-weather days inside," says the couple. The slim kitchen is the real deal, with a dark wooden benchtop to contrast the white cabinetry, tiled splash board, gas burner, magnetic knife strip, and the homiest of touches in the form of a sink, complete with filtered water and built from grandma's old enamel bowl. The look of the interior recalls a cozy,

Nordic cabin, paneled in wood and whitewashed, giving the illusion of a far greater space. "We wanted to achieve a rustic kind of look but not make the van super dark. I think we achieved that by mixing whites with browns and are super happy with how it turned out," they share. Indeed, when you stand in the kitchen, flanked by two wooden doors (behind which a toilet and wardrobe can be found), you can turn your head to look out the sizable window, set above a double bed, framing a new picturesque view each day. The van's original windows were part of the original pull, giving the interior views in every direction. Alongside the charming sink, it's the view from bed that Weigelt and Krüger cherish the most. "We always park with the prettiest view to the back of our van, so when we wake up, that's the first thing we see," they explain. Across from the kitchen, and fitted in behind the driver's seat, is an L-shaped seating area, with a sliding table that allows for easy access to the much-relied-upon storage contained in the seats. Inside, there is not only space for belongings, but for a refrigerator and their many electricals, which includes a solar-power system.

*Hot-air balloons take flight in Cappadocia, Turkey (opposite).*

Along the way, they've picked up another traveler, Luna, a rescue dog from Croatia, and adapted the interior to give her a storage nook underneath the bed to use as her own little home, from which she comes and goes as she pleases. Now, after a few years on the road, the memories are many, ranging from spending the night in the middle of Swedish woods in October to seeing the Northern Lights and experiencing snow chaos in Turkey, where the van lost control on a steep hill. It was a close call that nearly resulted in them sliding off the street, which didn't have any guardrails. So far, they have traversed much of Europe: Sweden, Norway, Finland, the Polish Baltic coast, Slovakia, Croatia, Bosnia, Romania, Albania, Greece, Turkey, Spain, and Portugal. With the pair committed to life on the road, the list is bound to go on. ∎

## DETAILED VEHICLE INFORMATION

The conversion of this Mercedes-Benz was led by the needs of full-time life on the road. Comfort and practicality were therefore key. Today it is solar powered and contains a water filtration system, a kitchenette with a gas stovetop, a sink, and ample space for food preparation. Sealed off by wooden doors from the main area are a wardrobe and toilet. The bed, at the far end of the van, is framed by a large, original window that offers the best view in the "house" of the changing landscapes outdoors.

| Manufacturer | MERCEDES-BENZ | Year | 1986 |
|---|---|---|---|
| Model | 407 D | Mileage | 103,340 KM (64,212 MI) |

Dinner night in the van (above). Looking out at the Lofoten Islands in Norway (opposite).

# The Modular Minivan That Can Do It All

On the outside, it may fool you as just another small-but-mighty 2009 Piaggio Porter Minivan, but housed inside is a space of no small wonder. The interior of the van has been fitted out by owner and designer Kerstin Bürk to have an ingenious, modular setup. The van, affectionately named Patscho, is the result of her final bachelor's project in Architecture. Her research into mobile living in small spaces was driven by contemporary issues of rising populations, high rental prices, and location-independent working. "As my final project, I did not just want to plan something, but also build and create a living space, which made me find and convert this little Piaggio Porter Minivan," says Bürk.

In length, there was just enough room for a bed inside. Bürk's challenge was to work with the confines of the space to create a functional and flexible small-scale mobile space, and all of this on a student budget, to boot. "Because of the tiny space, I decided to use multifunctions to create all the characteristics for a one-person rolling home. Patscho now works like a Swiss Army knife: multifunctional and compact at the same time," she says. "When the van is closed, it offers privacy and protection: there is a sleeping area and storage space in the form of adaptable shelving.

Patscho's functional modules can be easily changed by opening up, pulling, pushing, and folding, which you can do, for example, to set up the seats and table inside. Opening the van then creates new outdoor spaces: the tailgate folds out into a kitchen and living area, and offers additional protection from the rain when cooking, eating, or working outdoors, where there is plenty of room for social evenings with camper friends," explains Bürk. For more entertaining and stargazing, there's even a wooden rooftop terrace, and with practicality never far behind, a solar-powered shower, too.

Despite the project's goals for low-cost mobile living, the plan wasn't actually to live in Patscho long-term. But as it happened, Bürk ended up living in the van, proving what the design set out to do, and racking up adventures along the road. "The design means I can park and spend the night almost anywhere, whether in the middle of a city or a remote spot in the countryside. It worked out so well that I lived in it for two years, full-time. As a passionate surfer, it gave me the freedom to live anywhere along the Atlantic coastline and search for waves and adventures

Taking in Dakhla, Western Sahara *(opposite)*.

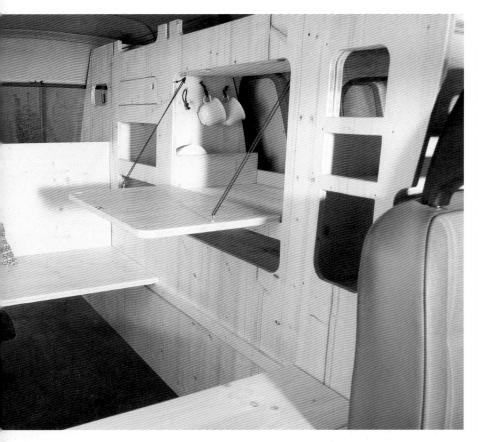

Patscho's multifunctional
modular interior *(opposite)*.
The pop-out breakfast
bar *(above left)*. A kitchen
with a view *(above right)*.

between Ireland and Morocco. Living only with the
bare essentials taught me a lot about what's really
important in life," she says. Along the way, she made
use of another of the wonder-van's multifunctions,
her so-called "rolling shop": from the van's pop-up-shop
terrace, she sold handmade jewelry and surf ponchos.
But of course it doesn't end there. There is one final
boon: to top it all off, the entire interior is also
removable, so that Patscho can also be used as a
regular transport vehicle to get from A to B. According
to Bürk, the whole modular interior can be removed
in less than ten minutes by two strong people. It's
a pretty strong case for modular-mobile living too. ■

## DETAILED VEHICLE INFORMATION

This 2009 Piaggio Porter Minivan underwent an
inspired, modular conversion that allows it to
function, as needed, as a home on the road, a shop,
or a regular transport vehicle. Inside is a sleeping
area, storage space, and a seating area, all accessed
via modular elements that can be opened up and
folded out. Outside, a kitchen and living area can
be folded out from the tailgate; there is a rooftop
"terrace," and even a solar-powered shower.

| Manu-facturer | PIAGGIO | Year | 2009 |
|---|---|---|---|
| Model | PORTER | Mileage | 107,000 KM (66,487 MI) |

# A Little Home for Big World Journeys

Switzerland-based couple Steven Streuli and Sandra Schönbächler might be relatively new to life on the road, but their converted 2015 Renault Master is more than ready for long-distance adventure, fitted out with all the comforting designs of an airy, well-designed home. The thought of traveling in a van had been on Schönbächler's mind for some time prior to their inaugural trip to Sardinia in May 2021. In early 2020, they decided they were ready for a new project, bought the van, named it Beavan, and began converting "him" in the fall of 2020 as their big winter project. Most of the build was done in four weeks and the rest found its way into their weekends.

"Our focus during the build was an open-space concept, with enough space for homey living and, especially, for living with our two little dogs Shira and Lio," says Streuli. To make it a reality, they enlisted the carpentry skills of Schönbächler's brother. Together, they successfully executed a cozy interior encased in a lightweight, practical van to travel in. Cozy, though, doesn't quite do Beavan's interior justice: behind the van's unassuming buttercup-yellow exterior lies a masterfully designed home. Looking at the images of the inside of the van, you could be fooled into thinking it was a petite apartment or part of the tiny house movement. Schönbächler's eye for interior design saw a forest-green kitchen installed, complete with light wooden benchtops, a spice rack, sink, and double burner, with plenty of space for preparing food, without the usual van issue of bumping into each other. Next to the kitchen, there's a relatively spacious seating area, containing built-in benches padded with cushions and throws in relaxing sandy shades, set around a square wooden table with views of the great outdoors—or wooden venetian blinds, should you want some privacy.

To the side of the kitchen, you'll find a small bathroom with shower and toilet, tiled in white and tastefully outfitted with black hardware. There is plenty of storage, as befitting life contained within four moving walls: little corners to store or place belongings, built to make use of the curvature of the van's shell, explain Schönbächler and Streuli. Plus, there's a uniquely elevated wooden bed frame that frees up extra space to move around inside.

Heading out on the road mid-pandemic was not without challenges: "We managed to get Covid-19

**Off-grid Beavan as seen from above (opposite).**

The dog balcony and dining area
beneath the elevated bed
*(opposite)*. The green kitchen to
rival a tiny home *(above left)*.
Resting companions *(above right)*.

during a trip to Tuscany. Because of the many
complicated responsibilities you have in a van: water,
toilet, shower, dogs, groceries, laundry—we decided
to drive home, not only for our sake but especially for
the dogs." The ailing pair drove the 10 hours home,
through a heat wave and without any air-conditioning.
"It was horrible. We really needed a van break after
that!" But if their first big trip to Sardinia is anything
to go by, there will certainly be more ahead. "We
went to Sardinia and really got to taste life in a van.
It was a mess, but we loved it so much. We had our
little home and the big world, just us and everything.
It was wild. We really met another world, a nature-
bound one; we saw wild pigs, dogs, cats, cows, donkeys,
and so much nature. After that, we made the decision
to travel for a longer period of time." ∎

## DETAILED VEHICLE INFORMATION

The Renault Master underwent a full conversion to
become a home on the road. The top priority was
keeping the vehicle as lightweight as possible, while
furnishing it with the most livable interior. The
cozy inside is more studio apartment than van cubby
and is full of creature comforts, including a sizable
kitchenette with wooden countertops, a bed, a seating
area, a toilet, and a shower. The space-saving design
includes ample storage and an elevated bed that frees
up floor space.

| Manu-facturer | RENAULT | Year | 2015 |
|---|---|---|---|
| Model | MASTER L3H2 | Mileage | 60,000 KM (37,282 MI) |

# In This Volkswagen Camper Van, the '70s Are Here to Stay

Amelia Le Brun's dream was to one day own a Volkswagen Westfalia Camper Van. The German maker's design, first issued in 1950, converted the iconic Volkswagen into a perfectly compact and affordable home on the road. As luck would have it, today Le Brun is the proud owner of a mustard-yellow number. Her camper van comes complete with huge, emblematic bay windows and a spare tire on the front, and remains a testament to both the model's history and durability. "Nothing of the van has been changed since she rolled out of the factory in '76," says Le Brun. The statement is far from hyperbole: the van has never even been resprayed, and turns heads on the road with its brilliantly '70s hue. The entirety of the original interior is also intact, recalling the nostalgic design of half a century ago. While on the outside it might look deceptively compact, the inside is efficiently kitted out and roomy, with the coziest of touches.

Up front, you roll along in tartan-style upholstered seats. When it's time to eat, there's a wood-paneled kitchenette, complete with a sink and an adjacent table. For sleeping, there's room for two or more—Le Brun's van also has the unique advantage of a pop-up top that makes space for an extra bed and brings you closer to starry nights. "I remember when I was looking, the pop-top was nonnegotiable. Now, whenever I pull up to camp and push the top up, it brings me so much joy, and I remember how lucky I am to own her," shares Le Brun.

Despite the camper van's seniority, even the engine is completely original. It's only able to speed up to a maximum of 96.5 kph (60 mph), but Le Brun has found it completely reliable for long-distance journeys all the same. In fact, the quirk just makes the van all the more special to her owner. "She has an air-cooled engine, with little going wrong, and less going wrong that I can't fix. This makes us incredibly self-sufficient as well as turning heads wherever we go!" says Le Brun, who prefers to do all repairs herself. So far, the VW has allowed Le Brun and her girlfriend, their two rescue dogs, and little van cat Dolly to explore the lush landscapes of England, Scotland, and Wales, camping by mountains and thicketed forests, cruising through postcard country lanes, and stopping off to surf remote, rugged coastlines. As with any

Driving through postcard villages *(opposite)*.

Details of the van's original '70s interior *(above left)*. Making the most of the pop-up top *(above right)*. Staying cozy with the rescue dogs *(right)*.

journey, there have been ups and downs, but one of the best experiences Le Brun describes was an unexpectedly joyous, yet freezing-cold week in Wales, on the road with their three furry companions, spending time hiking, camping, and wild swimming. "Despite the lack of heating, I loved this trip. It felt like the start of something new," says Le Brun. With a camper van that continues to stand the test of time, there are surely plenty more new experiences in store. "She has only had two owners, both of whom have treasured her, as I will as long as I have her," says Le Brun. ∎

## DETAILED VEHICLE INFORMATION

This Volkswagen T2 Van, manufactured in 1976, is completely intact and offers all the quirks of its original design, including Volkswagen's iconic bay windows and spare tire affixed to the front. The vans, at their time of make, were a top choice for a compact and economical van, each boasting a wood-paneled kitchenette, table, and seating and sleeping areas inside. This model includes a pop-up top, which creates space for an extra bed with elevated views outdoors.

| Manufacturer | VOLKSWAGEN | Year | 1976 |
|---|---|---|---|
| Model | T2 WESTFALIA | Mileage | 225,000 KM (140,000 MI) |

Taking in the ever-changing landscape views *(above)*.

# Rugged Sites and Local Lore in Great Britain

*Julia Nimke traveled through England and Scotland in search of its folklore, finding tales of the occult in its most rugged, and fittingly mystical, landscapes.*

**Great Britain** | In July 2018, photographer Julia Nimke set off on a unique trip through Great Britain's vast national parks on a route led not by maps but by fables. The trip was part of a year-long photographic research project, *Folk Tales,* that took her across Europe to document sites and stories of lore. "I wanted to drive through England, Wales, and Scotland and take in as much of the natural beauty as possible," says Nimke. "I am a huge lover of remote places and the road less traveled."

Though temperate, Great Britain's climes are known to be temperamental too. "I've always had a thing for rough landscapes, rainy weather, and the U.K.," she says. As such, she was prepared for the worst. "Layers are king. I took mainly outdoor clothing with me as I knew I wanted to spend as much time as possible hiking and exploring places by foot." But the trip proved otherwise, with the kind of mild weather conditions largely unheard of in the British summer. "I was surprised how little it rained! I'd say 80 percent of the time it was sunny. I guess I was pretty lucky," says Nimke.

Arriving at the port of Dover in her cozy Mercedes-Benz Sprinter, one of Nimke's first stops was Stonehenge. The 4,600-year-old monument's beginnings are still shrouded in mystery: one of many legends tells of Merlin magicking the stones over from Scotland. Next, Nimke drove northeast through Bristol and up into Wales to visit the vast Brecon Beacons National Park. Beloved for hiking, it is home to four mountain ranges, including the ancient woodland of upland Fforest Fawr, a UNESCO Global Geopark and International Dark Sky Reserve (one of only 20 in the world, and offering unparalleled starry nights).

In between sites, Nimke would document her findings from the comfort of her van. "It was the perfect home for me. We were a good team already from a ton of trips in the previous months and years... I don't need a lot of comfort and luxury. A good mattress, some space to store things, and a table to work at from time to time is all I really need," she shares.

From the Brecon Beacons, Nimke journeyed northwest to the Welsh island of Anglesey, long linked to the magical order of the Druids, whose sorcery is said to have fronted the Celtic defense against the Romans.

Then it was back to England, to the Peak District, whose geography is characterized by moorlands, limestone gorges, and valleys, and rich cultural history, too. Lud's Church, to name just one site, is a mysterious gorge that runs 17 meters (56 feet) deep and 100 meters (328 feet) long. Believed to be an early Pagan site of worship, to this day, on summer solstice, the sun shines straight into the gorge at the stroke of midday. Next, it was onwards to the rugged mountains and glacial ribbon lakes of the Lake District in Cumbria, home to England's largest and deepest natural lakes and Neolithic stone formations, including "Long Meg and Her Daughters," which legends tell us are witches, petrified mid-dance.

Nimke closed her research trip in Scotland, driving first to the capital, Edinburgh, and then into the wildly beautiful Scottish Highlands, one of the most sparsely populated areas in Europe. Along the road, as a solo traveler and researcher, interacting with locals and travelers alike became the highlight of her trip. "Especially when you travel alone, you are a lot more open to engaging with people... Also, for my project, it was essential to talk to people and to find people that wanted to tell me tales from the past," she says.

From Inverness, Nimke drove over to the picturesque Isle of Skye, a land dense with folklore that includes mythical creatures like fairies, who lend their name to various geological forms, and Old Man of Storr, one of the sites Nimke was most curious to visit. The 49-meter (160-foot) pinnacle rock formation is said to be the giant Old Man of Storr laid to rest. A hike up

Breathtaking seaside cliffs *(opposite).*

Old Man of Storr
Isle of Skye

Inverness

SCOTLAND

Glencoe

Edinburgh

GREAT
BRITAIN

Long Meg and
Her Daughters

ENGLAND

Lud's Church

IRELAND

Anglesey

Brecon Beacons
National Park

Bristol

Stonehenge

Dover

FRANCE

**Parking up by the water (above). A remote house on the moors (right).**

to this wondrous site, set on a ridge, offers panoramic views of the sea and the mainland.

The last stop on her route was Glencoe, set in the Scottish Highlands, with its dramatic valleys and mountains formed by glaciers and volcanic activity. It is famed for its otherworldly landscapes and is also home to a thatched-roofed Folk Museum dedicated to preserving the area's cultural history.

As an experienced vanlifer, Nimke is full of advice for a magical trip. "Leave space for surprises. It's nice to check and do research before heading out for a trip. But, I think the magic of traveling, though, is finding places that you haven't seen a photo of before." ∎

Looking out into the wilderness
(top). The otherworldly Isle of
Skye, Scotland (above). Seagulls
perch (right). Winding through
the verdant Scottish landscape
(opposite).

# A Flower Power Camper Fit for Adventure

Amelia Fitzpatrick bought her beloved van when she was still in college and beginning to ponder how life would look post-graduation. "I had a dream of driving to California and moving out there, but I couldn't afford rent and a car," she explains. The answer? A 1977 Volkswagen T2 Westfalia. "I thought it would be the most financially secure venture, and would provide me with both a safe place to sleep and wheels to get around."

California, birthplace of the peace-promoting flower-power movement, would prove the perfect setting for Fitzpatrick's bus, with its sage-green exterior decorated with daisies. In advertisements published at the time of its release, the 1977 Volkswagen T2 Westfalia, part of the iconic 50 year collaboration between Volkswagen and Westfalia, was billed as perhaps "the most civilized recreational vehicle ever." It was designed "to carry your big family and all its gear to and from home," while doubling as a "home away from home" for vacationing.

Its interior, meanwhile, boasted "everything, including the kitchen sink," as Fitzpatrick's vehicle, which has retained its original layout, attests. The inside includes a built-in kitchen area, with the aforementioned sink, a gas stove, an icebox, a water pump, and a fold-out dining table. Other features include a comfortable sofa, which pulls out to form the lower half of the van's principal double bed, and shelves for storage. Then there is the van's pop-up top, which creates valuable added height in seconds and houses a small mezzanine area that can function as a single bed. This feature is Fitzpatrick's favorite part of the bus. "When you're living in a small space, I think it is critical to be able to stand up inside, so you don't lose your mind," she says. "I also love that the bed up top folds out, because sleeping up there is the best: a cool breeze and a great view of the stars."

Fitzpatrick's interior decor is in keeping with the bohemian spirit of the Volkswagen's exterior, from the decorative floral rug that lines the floor to the mandala-patterned fabric that adorns the ceiling, framing an elegant lantern at its center. "There isn't anything too unique about my bus versus other buses," says Fitzpatrick, "apart from that little chandelier, which I made. I think it's a nice touch." Other details include wooden paneling, rust-orange curtains that

Overlooking the Anza-Borrego Desert State Park, California, USA (opposite).

Waking up on the beach, California (opposite). The cozy, textural interior (above left). Adventuring in California (above right).

match the van's plaid upholstery, olive-green cabinet fittings in keeping with the 1970s color palette, and a striped sofa cover in the same earthy hues.

Fitzpatrick has ventured all around the United States in her trusty van, from the deserts of Utah to the mountains of southern Georgia. She has faced trials and triumphs along the way, and describes the highs and lows of vanlife as being indelibly connected. When her van broke down atop the Rocky Mountains, for instance, the panic that ensued was matched by "the pure joy of riding down the other side into Utah" once the vehicle was back up and running.

Likewise, when the bus's battery died in the middle of the desert, without another human being in sight, Fitzpatrick had to think fast to work out a means of charging it on her own. "Nothing can match the feeling of accomplishment of getting yourself out of a sticky situation. I honestly think I live for the challenges. That is why almost every 'worst' moment is equally one of my best—these are things that have ultimately shaped who I am, and my relationship with my van." ∎

## DETAILED VEHICLE INFORMATION

Designed as a recreational family vehicle, its attractive exterior, fuel-injected two-liter engine, and nifty use of space—it comes with a fully equipped kitchen and can sleep two adults and three children—rendered it a timeless classic.

| Manu-facturer | VOLKSWAGEN | Year | 1977 |
|---|---|---|---|
| Model | T2 WESTFALIA | Mileage | 177,000 KM (110,000 MI) |

# A Folkloric House Truck, Hewn by Hand

In 2010, at a second-hand bookstore, Kai Watkins picked up a copy of *Some Turtles Have Nice Shells,* a book that chronicled unique house trucks built as a part of the hippie movement of the '60s and '70s. Leafing through the vivid imagery of fantastical, woodworked trucks, she found inspiration for a new way of living. "I immediately thought that I wanted to build one someday, but as I was in my early 20s, I didn't have the money or skills to start a project like that," she says. The idea, however, stuck. Seeking an alternative to prohibitively priced land in her area, she eventually took up carpentry night classes and saved as much as she could for her dream project. By 2013, she was the owner of an International 3800 and began the slow, but fruitful building process.

Watkins lived on a commune for several summers, where she collaborated on truck builds alongside others in search of an alternative lifestyle. "It was nice to have a community of other young people who were all figuring out how to live in tiny mobile structures. We would have parties and potlucks, bonfires in the field, group building projects. It was always good to have someone around to lend a hand," she shares. Watkin's design is inspired by what she calls British Columbia's

West Coast craftsmanship: the small logger and fisherman cabins, built with hand-split cedar shakes (like shingles but hand ripped as opposed to cut) and reclaimed materials, many of which she collected during her travels in her 20s. "I wanted to use as many local and salvaged materials as possible, so, for example, the roof and walls are covered in hand-split cedar shakes, from cedar that I found on the beach and bucked up with a chainsaw, then split with a mallet and froe," she explains. The result is an exterior that feels very much like a cabin on wheels, with the wooden shakes encasing the home like, say, a turtle shell. "You don't see many road rigs covered in cedar shakes, and everyone always asks if they fall off on the highway, but I haven't ever lost any!" says Watkins of the truck.

The van's exterior is inspired by British Columbia's West Coast craftsmanship *(opposite).*

To reach the interior, you come up a quaint back porch that is also inspired by history: "The whole idea of having a back porch just seems very romantic, like an old Romani cart or a covered wagon," says Watkins. Then it's through a curved wooden door, fitted with panes of likewise curved glass. Inside, the visual effect

Peering inside from the wooden porch *(opposite)*. Washing dishes, always with a view *(above left)*. One half of the wooden galley kitchen *(above right)*.

of different wood types and old-world touches is immediately warming.

"I'm a woodworker and like using all endemic wood species of my province. So, every piece of wood on the truck was logged from the forests around here, and I can identify them all," says Watkins. Salvaged materials used in the build include windows from a century-old house and light switches that are even older. There's a large circular window over a bench that looks made for reading and daydreaming, a forest-green wood-burning stove in a tiled alcove, and a functional, compact kitchen complete with an oven and porcelain sink. On the inside and out, the overall effect is singular and almost folkloric, like something you could imagine illustrated in a storybook. "I wanted it to feel like a structure that had been around for a very long time, like a Baba Yaga's hut. I always envisioned the house truck as a squatter cabin on wheels, so we can drift around the province and live in different beautiful places," says Watkins. ∎

## DETAILED VEHICLE INFORMATION

A carpentry-led conversion, using local wood species and architectural quirks, has transformed a truck into a cabin-on-the-road that references the house truck movement. The outer shell features hand-split cedar shakes and a back porch, while the inside offers the comforts of a galley-style wooden kitchen, complete with a fridge, stovetop, oven, and a large porcelain sink with a view. Adjacent to it, an antique wood-burning stove keeps the interior warm and cozy.

| Manu-facturer | NAVISTAR | Year | 1992 |
|---|---|---|---|
| Model | INTERNATIO-NAL 3800 | Mileage | 380,000 KM (236,000 MI) |

# A Sustainable Solution for Slow, Wild Living

In 2018, propelled by a desire to own their first home and experience travel on a full-time basis, American partners Fiorella Yriberry and Zach Macaluso purchased a 2003 Ford E−450 shuttle bus, with a 27-passenger capacity, for $5,000. Shortly after, they began the process of reconstructing it as a tiny home on wheels. This took two years in total, costing the pair another $5,000. "The design and style of the bus were influenced by our urge to do something different on a low budget while honoring our bohemian aesthetic," they explain. "We focused on building sustainably with as little waste as possible, using mostly second-hand materials."

They named the bus Luna and repainted its white exterior with a combination of white and mustard-yellow, setting the tone for their bohemian vision. "We love how different it is," they enthuse of the paint job. "Both the colors and how it represents our personality." When it came to the interior layout, meanwhile, their biggest concern was retaining an open floor plan. "We are keen yogis and wanted to make sure we had a hallway large enough for two yoga mats, so we could practice together inside on chilly mornings or rainy days."

They were also determined to exploit the influx of natural light, courtesy of the bus's many expansive windows—one of their favorite things about it. "We wanted the interior to feel big and bright, so we avoided large overhead cabinets and used a sliding barn door for the bathroom entrance," the couple expands. Vintage details abound, from the duo's striking black laboratory sink to their rustic kitchen cabinet doors, while the color palette ranges from warm wood tones to white and sage-green paintwork. The interior's organic feel is enhanced by the inclusion of natural detailing, including wicker lampshades, a wonky piece of wood that hangs over their double bed at the bus's rear ("our famous decor stick!"), and their use of twigs for drawer handles—plus plenty of plants.

**The cheerfully hued van parked in fresh forest snow (opposite).**

"The emphasis on sustainability and sourcing secondhand enabled us to create a unique and eclectic space with its own personality," they say of what makes Luna so special. Another singular feature is their gravity-fed solar shower. "We opted for simple plumbing and ended up creating this shower with a combination of different elements," they explain. "We have never seen one like it before, and it works like a charm!"

View from driver's seat *(above left)*. Bison grazing out the window *(above right)*. The cozy wooden interior is accented with calming pops of sage *(right)*.

In their two years on the road, Yriberry and Macaluso have traveled far and wide in their covetable motor home, visiting Washington, South Dakota, the Grand Tetons, and Yellowstone National Park, among other U.S. destinations, and exploring parts of Mexico, too. They've had one or two hitches along the way, including losing the lug nuts from one of their rear tires while driving on the highway—"that was very scary." Overall, however, their adventures so far have proved both liberating and nourishing. "Our best experiences are calling so many secluded and beautiful locations home. There's nothing better for us than to be living a simple slow life with Luna in the wild." ■

# DETAILED VEHICLE INFORMATION

Often starting life as a school or city bus, the Ford E–450, with its long, lofty interior, is an optimum base for camper conversion, offering plenty of space and potential for customization. Yriberry and Macaluso have made wonderful use of their E–450 chassis, creating a covetable interior defined by natural materials and earthy tones. This, coupled with its impressive windows, creates a pleasing synergy between indoors and out, ideal for a duo whose self-proclaimed goal is living life "slow and wild."

| Manufacturer | FORD | Year | 2003 |
|---|---|---|---|
| Model | E – 450 | Mileage | MORE THAN 240,000 KM (150,000 MI) |

The couple prioritized second-hand materials to create their "eclectic, boho space" *(above)*.

# A Commercial Van Turned Covetable Home

Partners Tarn Soden and Reece Markham first felt the pull of the open road when their plans to travel overseas were thwarted by the Covid-19 pandemic. They purchased a white Iveco Daily 50C17, a large, light commercial van, and resolved to turn it "into a home that could be with us wherever we traveled," they explain. "We designed and built the entire setup ourselves and, after a lot of blood, sweat, and tears, were beyond amazed by the final product," says Soden.

When planning the build, the couple's main priority was creating a pleasant space to truly live in. "We knew we wanted to spend a few good years traveling in our van, so we needed it to feel as much like a 'home' on wheels as possible," says Soden. For them, this meant installing a sizable kitchen to aid their love of cooking, as well as an office/living area that would enable them to work remotely or relax as required. "Iveco Dailys are slightly wider than most vans of a similar size, which meant we were able to fit a double mattress in widthways," says Soden. This, she notes, was key when it came to incorporating a more open and spacious living area.

The pair has an evident flair for design and, eight months after starting the task, their van—which they named Oakie—looked every part the miniature apartment. The interior is painted predominantly white, with a pale wooden ceiling and floorboards, and a kitchen countertop in darker wood fitted with a Thetford gas stovetop. A sleek black Bushman fridge, elegant rattan-fronted storage cabinets, cotton and linen fabrics, and a series of colorfully patterned throws complete the effect. "We believed that by incorporating our own taste and style into every element of our van build, we would create a unique and beautiful setup," they say. "Things like the glass jars on our upper kitchen shelf—yes, they stay there while we drive: heavy-duty Velcro is the best—to our plants, ukulele and guilele, and the spice rack Tarn's dad built for her when she was young: it has all come together so nicely."

Markham's favorite detail is the large under-bed storage area that they've dubbed "the garage"—"it can hold all of our diving, hiking, and outdoor gear including two surfboards"—while Soden delights in the calming kitchen, which inspires her to dream up new recipes, as well as natural home and skin-care products from scratch.

Oakie and his friends parking by the sea (opposite).

A sunny reading spot in bed (*above left*). A musical moment (*above right*). The kitchen's spice rack, built by Soden's dad (*right*).

In their 18 months of traveling in Oakie, the duo has ventured all around Australia. "We have had so many incredible experiences in the van that it's too hard to name the best, but the thing we've loved the most about this lifestyle is the beautiful people we've met along the way," they say. "The vanlife community is so supportive and welcoming." When it comes to less enjoyable experiences, however, there are very few of note. "We have been lucky enough that nothing 'bad' really stands out," says Soden. "I will say the everyday tasks like filling up your water tanks, showering, cooking, cleaning, shopping, and even finding a safe place to sleep can feel exhausting at times." But that hasn't deterred them in the slightest: "we're looking to ship Oakie to New Zealand in the next year or so," they enthuse of their plans for more vanlife exploits. ∎

## DETAILED VEHICLE INFORMATION

Dating back to 1978, the Iveco Daily makes a brilliant base for van conversions thanks to both its long wheelbase and vast loading space, which allow for endless layout options. Designed to carry heavy cargo, the Daily is equipped with a powerful-enough engine to bear a well-decked home on wheels, while its build is sturdy enough to endure extreme off-roading antics. Soden and Markham have made good use of their capacious commercial van, installing plenty of hidden storage to house all their adventuring gear.

| Manufacturer | IVECO | Year | 2014 |
|---|---|---|---|
| Model | DAILY 50C17 | Mileage | 110,000 KM (68,351 MI) |

The homey whitewashed interior includes a full double bed with hidden storage (above).

# The Versatile Sprinter Designed for Play

German couple Frank Stoll and Selina Mei first felt the pull of vanlife while touring Australia in 2016. When they returned to Europe, they decided to invest in a van of their own, purchasing a Volkswagen Transporter (T4) on eBay and transforming it into their dream home on wheels. Fast forward a few years and they were joined by their baby son Fiete, now two, and decided it was time to upsize. "We decided to build a bigger van," the pair explains. "So, we bought a 2015 Mercedes Sprinter 316, which we named Bruno, to create the perfect travel setup for the three of us."

Sprinters are a popular choice when it comes to conversion bases, thanks to their versatile, cavernous interiors and sturdy build. "When we bought it, it was just a big white box without any features," they say. Having honed their van construction skills during their previous build, however, the duo was well versed in conjuring up a bespoke living space for family life on the road.

"It's taken us roughly one year to get where we are now," they explain, "which is a fully equipped camper van, including windows, which we've built entirely on our own." Bruno's exterior features a white upper body, while its lower section is a deep green topped by khaki and tangerine stripes, inspired by a 1970s aesthetic. "We wanted to give the van a unique overlander style even though it's a two-wheel drive." The inside, meanwhile, a combination of bright-white walls and pale laminated wood crafted from ilomba and poplar, is a masterclass in space maximization. "We wanted to make a space where we could all have a good time in any conditions," the couple explains.

At the rear sits a large seating and dining area, elevated by a series of drawers that provide plenty of storage space. This transforms niftily into the family's sleep zone, made up of a row of long sleepers. The front of the van hosts a roomy kitchen, complete with a sink and large refrigerator, a wooden countertop with terrazzo upsides, plus more storage units. "The kitchen unit is our favorite part of the van, both in how it looks and how it functions," says the pair. "We also have an integrated toilet hidden away, which is useful."

The interior also boasts plenty of floor space for Fiete to play on, and he even has his own swing, which attaches to the roof rack and allows him to sway

*The family enjoys a playful moment (opposite).*

Misty morning views *(above left)*. The airy interior is a masterclass in storage *(above right)*. The rear drawer kitchen *(right)*.

in the van's entrance. "We got him a slide, too, so that he can enter and exit the van on his own, as it's pretty high," his parents add.

At the back of the vehicle, a pull-out seat gives Mei and Stoll their own opportunity for relaxation, while a wood-paneled roof terrace provides a platform from which to appreciate their surroundings. So far, the family and Bruno have traveled through Germany, Austria, Switzerland, Italy, Slovenia, and Croatia, documenting their picturesque journeys—and the various stages of their van conversion process—on their envy-inducing Instagram account.

"We haven't had any best or worst experiences in Bruno yet," say Mei and Stoll, which perhaps is not surprising, given how recently they completed the van's metamorphosis. "We just love being on the road and discovering the world in our very own way." ∎

## DETAILED VEHICLE INFORMATION

Sprinters are the ideal vehicle for imaginative vanlifers looking to build their own van home from scratch. Their lofty interiors allow for all kinds of layout options, while this edition's CDI engine provides excellent fuel mileage. Mei and Stoll have rendered their 316 entirely their own: a family-friendly van with inventive customizations, from a detachable play swing to a convertible sitting/dining/sleeping area, housing multiple storage spaces accessible from the top or back of the van.

| Manufacturer | MERCEDES-BENZ | Year | 2015 |
|---|---|---|---|
| Model | SPRINTER 316 CDI L2H2 | Mileage | 170,000 KM (105,633 MI) |

Coastal dining on nature's porch (*above*).

# Retracing the Silk Road in Georgia

*To discover if vestiges of the ancient pathway still exist today, Milene van Arendonk and Yuri Jones set off along the Silk Road in their beloved VW.*

**Georgia** | As part of an extensive journey to retrace the Silk Road, Milene van Arendonk and Yuri Jones traveled through Georgia in their 45-year-old Volkswagen van, Alexine, named after the Dutch explorer Alexine Tinne. The pair began their trip in March 2021, setting off from The Hague in the Netherlands. At the time of writing, they are in Iran. "We are driving along the Silk Road to try to search for places that still have traces of the ancient road, like the last silkworm farm in Georgia," shares the ambitious team. Reaching back to the first century BCE, the Silk Road was a network of trade pathways used for roughly 1,500 years, connecting Asia with Europe and sweeping through Central Asia and the Middle East.

For the couple, it was a book about Marco Polo that started it all. "It was not so much him that interested me but the road: an ancient road that still influences today, a road that not only people traveled on but also products, cultures, diseases," van Arendonk explains. "I wanted to see and experience what was left of this ancient road and how it precisely influenced the modern world."

Georgia, at the intersection of East and West, hosts many important Silk Road stops and abundant natural wonders. "The incredible Georgian nature blew our minds," say Van Arendonk and Jones. Among their many stops, the pair ventured to the vertiginous 14th-century Trinity Church in Kazbegi, experienced the Abano Pass (one of the highest thoroughfares in the Caucasus Mountains), the canyons and peaks of Vashlovani National Park in eastern Georgia, the city of Sighnaghi, an ancient stop on the Silk Road, and Vardzia, a cave city dating back to the 12th century, built as a safe haven against invaders. Traveling onwards, in northwest Georgia, they visited the city of Ushguli with its famous defensive towers, the lakes and mountains of Mestia, and the former Soviet spa of Tskaltubo in west-central Georgia.

Besides local history, in a 45-year-old Persian-inspired turquoise VW, many other lessons were learned along the way. "Our van is the most fantastic home on the road," the couple explains. "We kept her very basic, thus: no kitchen, toilet, or space to stand up. The only thing we have is a couch which becomes a bed and some cabinets." But despite her reliability as a home, her age and make—not to mention an unexpected heat wave in the usually mild summer—brought challenges along dusty Georgian roads. Therefore, she is not used to and doesn't like hot dusty weather. We did a mechanic course before starting our journey, but the real course we got was on the road."

Georgia proved particularly challenging, but a breakdown led to their lasting connections with an unexpected community of local VW enthusiasts. "In Georgia … she bravely managed to drive the most dangerous road of the country but broke down in the desert … Unfortunately, the country doesn't have any spare parts fit for a German car, but luckily, we found the VW van club of Georgia and became very good friends," they explain. "They were amazing, helping out with everything, and we fixed her in no time." The experience has left them as optimistic as ever and proved their ethos of finding growth through adversity. "With an old-timer [vintage car] you never know—things break down all the time, but the good thing is that it adds to the adventure."

Looking back on their journey so far, the pair is most grateful for the support and companionship they found from locals along their way. "We met so many people who helped us, cheered us on, and invited us in. They show that the Silk Road, on which the travelers really relied on the kindness of others, is still there," they share. "Traveling from one place to the other is easy, but traveling unknown roads not knowing where one will end up—because of the hurdles on the way—is something else. We got stuck sometimes

The historic town of Ushguli, Georgia *(opposite).*

A shrine on the way
to the Trinity Church in
mountainous Kazbegi
*(opposite)*. Skirting one of
Georgia's alpine lakes
*(above)*. Resting, come
golden hour *(left)*.

and had to be towed by strangers; we got lost now and
then and were invited for a cup of tea to figure out
where to go next, and when our van broke down, people
rushed over to help us out." Their discovery saw
them come full circle, back to the famous explorer who
inspired their trip. "We can only imagine that's
what Marco Polo went through as well, when not a
bumpy road but a sandstorm blocked his route,
not his van but his camel that didn't want to go further,
not the border control, but bandits who forced him
to take a different route," they muse. ∎

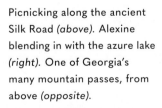

Picnicking along the ancient Silk Road (*above*). Alexine blending in with the azure lake (*right*). One of Georgia's many mountain passes, from above (*opposite*).

# A Spacious Former School Bus for Family Forays

Husband and wife duo Ben and Mande Tucker decided to embark upon vanlife in 2016, fueled by their shared sense of adventure and appreciation for the outdoors. It didn't take them long to find the perfect vehicle—a 1992 Navistar International 3800, with minimum rust and surprisingly low mileage, that they named Fern. Ben, who had already renovated a school bus with some friends several years earlier, was well-equipped for the task, and he and Mande eagerly set about transforming Fern into a traveling home.

The conversion took a year to complete, the couple explains, a process that involved painting the bright yellow exterior a fresh mint green and white, and gutting the interior "to take the school out of the school bus." Now, the inside is unrecognizable: a "roomy and comfortable" living zone made up of white-painted pine and natural cedar, along with acacia wood floors, copper curtain rods, butcher-block countertops, and live-edge lumber accents. The bus's capacious interior has proved particularly necessary with the passage of time, as the Michigan-based couple now have two children, Sawyer, four, and Eden, one, who accompany them on endless camping trips.

"As we grow older, time seems to be flying by at an increasingly rapid rate," the Tuckers explain. "Habits and routines can sometimes contribute to this time warp, so building and traveling in the bus has been our deliberate decision to shake things up, switch gears, and shift momentum in a new direction. With this lifestyle, we strive to live simply and within our means, so we can afford to pick up and travel when time allows."

Having kids has meant that the adventurous pair have had to curb their spontaneity and establish more of a routine on the road. "We have organized systems and a place for everything," they say. This includes "using up every last square inch" of Fern's 23.2-square-meter (250-square-foot) living space, with its rear sleeping section, neat kitchen, and upholstered seating area with plenty of hidden storage. "Both kids have cozy beds that can be tucked away during the day," the couple adds, "and snacks are always kept easily accessible."

In recent years, Fern and the Tuckers have ventured "through the Badlands and Black Hills of South Dakota," to Utah, Wyoming, Montana, and beyond. Highlights have included "hiking on glaciers

The van's roof rack doubles as a terrace and panoramic viewpoint (opposite).

Pine, cedar, and acacia wood warm up the interior (opposite). Mountain views from bed (above left). The former school bus is unrecognizable inside (above right).

and paddleboarding alongside a pair of loons in a hidden lake in the Canadian Rockies," and seeing "the magical landscape of Yellowstone National Park." The pair's electric bikes, which they hang from a rear fork mount when traveling, provide them with another means of transport once the bus is parked, while a cedar roof deck houses their paddleboards, and doubles as a space for "picnics and stargazing." They've even installed a series of removable posts that allow them to hang hammocks over the elevated platform.

Fern is fitted with a large diesel engine that the Tuckers describe as a "steady workhorse." They won't be winning any races in her, they joke, but she and their children have taught them the value of slow, appreciative travel. "We find ourselves more in the moment and seeking contentment in our surroundings," they note. "As a family, we dream of having more campfires, seeing more sunrises, swimming in mountain streams, seeing our country, and getting to know its people. And, with Fern's low mileage and solid condition, we hope we'll be traveling around with her for decades to come." ■

## DETAILED VEHICLE INFORMATION

Made after Navistar International took over International Harvester (IH), Fern is a second-generation S-series school bus. A redesign of the IH Schoolmaster, the new buses featured more aerodynamic exteriors, while their insides remained just as roomy, rendering them ripe for camper conversion. Fern's five-speed manual transmission offers greater control, while her naturally aspirated, mechanically injected engine is known for its reliability and longevity—a faithful steed for slow family travel.

| Manu-facturer | NAVISTAR | Year | 1992 |
|---|---|---|---|
| Model | INTERNATIO-NAL 3800 | Mileage | 75,640 KM (47,000 MI) |

# A Streamlined SUV Built for West Coast Adventures

Five years ago, Taylor May and her family sold their home and all of their belongings to travel full-time. Before they hit the road, they purchased a Toyota 4Runner. "We started without any fancy gear because we just wanted to be out exploring as much as possible. Over time, our experience has grown. We spend longer amounts of time out exploring, so our build has progressed to meet those needs," explains May. Their streamlined design, tweaked over the years with the mechanical skill of May's husband, is fit for long-distance travel and camp-style living, with a pop-up tent atop the vehicle for sleeping. "We built the 4Runner to be able to travel a lot of road miles, but it was also important for us to be able to access more remote campsites in the backcountry. It's the perfect mix of both worlds," says May. "We can travel cross-country and then be able to spend as many nights as we want to, completely self-sufficient in the middle of the desert or mountains."

Simplicity was key in the design, which includes cheerful yellow accents in the window stripes, equipment, and a pop-up tent. "I'm a minimalist when it comes to camping, mostly because I want to enjoy being outside rather than messing around with a huge tent or in-depth kitchen set up," says May who, in all

weather, can be found rustling up food from a pull-out prep drawer and countertop at the rear of the vehicle or flipping tortillas on a portable outdoor grill while enjoying the views. Given the petite quarters of their setup, life on the road has taught many lessons in small-space living. "My favorite feature is the drawer system. Organization on the road is key, something I learned early on. It's so nice to pull into camp and have everything you need easily accessible," she says.

Over the years, May has inevitably become an expert in traversing different terrains across the West Coast, with some lessons learned more harshly than others—like the time the family got stuck in the snow in California. "We were driving up to look at some mountain lakes for the day, and I was still inexperienced, and not prepared, and pushed my luck. We ended up driving farther than we should have into some deep snow and had to dig ourselves out before we could head back down the mountain," she says. "After that, I purchased reliable recovery gear to always have on hand! It was a good lesson in being prepared and knowing your vehicle and skill level."

Looking out on Mount Washington, Oregon, USA (opposite).

Skirting mountain ranges
*(above left)*. Stopping to
make lunch in the Alvord
Desert, Oregon, USA
*(above right)*. Camping
in the snow near Austin,
Nevada, USA *(right)*.

The family's travel schedule has changed over the
years. These days, May tends to be the chief adventurer,
heading out with the couple's two boys through the
West Coast's varied landscapes to experience desert
plains, secluded lakes, lush forests, and beyond.
"Our rig has taken us to some of the most unbelievable
places here in the U.S. I think anytime you can open
your tent window to a stunning sunrise or soak in a good
campfire, and really just appreciate being where you
are, it's wonderful. Not everyone has the ability to make
that happen; I've been lucky enough to experience
quite a few of those moments," she says. ■

## DETAILED VEHICLE INFORMATION

The Toyota 4Runner was chosen for its compact, off-road ability. Rather than fully converting the model, as many often do, the vehicle has had minimal renovations to keep travel on the road as streamlined as possible, maximizing time spent outdoors. A drawer system, fitted into the back of the vehicle, keeps belongings and supplies organized while traveling and can be used as a fold-out food preparation area next to a portable grill.

| Manufacturer | TOYOTA | Year | 2018 |
| --- | --- | --- | --- |
| Model | 4RUNNER SR5 | Mileage | 214,252 KM (133,130 MI) |

Sunrise from the pop-up tent, Eastern Oregon, USA *(above)*.

# A Blue Bulli Conversion with Standout Stripes

Swiss vanlifer Jsa Schwager bought her 1974 Volkswagen T2b bus (or "Bulli" as they're known in German) 14 years ago. "It had been in the previous owner's possession for a long time," she says. "I think I'm its third or fourth owner."

The bus has a striking royal-blue exterior with two blue stripes, in paler shades, that extend across its center in tiers: a suitably '70s aesthetic. "The retro stripes are really unique," says Schwager. "There's no other bus that looks like this one. It makes the van stand out, and people often give me a smile or a thumbs-up on the road."

Its interior, meanwhile, has been converted. "The last owner removed the original Westfalia setup, which is a pity," Schwager explains. "However, I like the conversion much better: it has so much more storage space, which is essential when you're on the road for a long time." When Schwager purchased the van, its floors and walls were carpeted. "The first thing I did was remove that, and then recarpeted, repainted, and refurbished," she says.

Now the bus has a warm, homey interior in cream and wood, with cerulean-blue upholstery to match its outer shell. "The seating area means that when it rains,

you can sit and eat comfortably," she notes. "And if it's raining heavily, you can then transform the dining area into a bed and sleep there too." On milder nights, however, Schwager sleeps in the Bulli's pop-top—that classic Westfalia feature—which houses a second raised bed. "The fact that there are two beds in the van is my favorite thing about it," she adds.

She also loves the Bulli's blue-and-white-striped awning, a feature she created herself. Extending out from the van's side, the simple but effective design is held aloft by three poles creating a makeshift porch in front of the vehicle's entrance and interior kitchen space. Schwager then sets up a table and chairs beneath the canopy to dine outdoors on warmer days. "In my eyes, the awning is a great feature," she enthuses. "I am very proud of how it turned out—and it really adds to the 1970s vibe."

A keen advocate of vanlife, Schwager set up her own company, Van Retreats, during the pandemic to share the joys of off-grid living. The retreats offer fellow van owners (or renters) the chance to engage in daily yoga or Pilates sessions in remote settings—an

*Setting up camp at the foot of the mountains (opposite).*

opportunity to "leave behind the noise and stress of everyday life and enjoy a simpler lifestyle in harmony with nature."

When she isn't leading a retreat, Schwager can frequently be found adventuring in her treasured Bulli. Together, they've explored Switzerland, Austria, Germany, France, Italy, the Netherlands, Belgium, Luxembourg, and Croatia, and have only broken down twice thus far. "That's not a bad record over the course of 14 years, especially given that the bus is so old," she says. Her most trying experience to date occurred when the van got stuck in a muddy field. "But, as is so often the case, there were a lot of friendly people around willing to help!" ∎

## DETAILED VEHICLE INFORMATION

Schwager's Volkswagen T2b bus stands out from the crowd with its striped paint job and converted interior, which sees the classic Westfalia setting replaced by a more spacious arrangement. The Type 2's pop-top creates valuable height and extra sleeping space, while Schwager's handmade blue-and-white-striped awning creates a charming alfresco dining area alongside the van's entrance. A front spare-tire mount completes the 1970s feel, while a rear mount makes for easy mountain bike storage.

| Manufacturer | VOLKSWAGEN | Year | 1974 |
|---|---|---|---|
| Model | T2B | Mileage | 349,228 KM (217,000 MI) |

The handy pop-up top bedroom is a space saver with a view (*above*). The van's awning and string lights set up in the golden hours (*opposite*).

# A Multifunctional Mercedes that Looks Marvelous

German partners Zoé Hopfstock and Oscar Simon began dreaming of life on the road while at university in Düsseldorf, where they studied architecture and mechanical engineering, respectively. "We knew we wanted to explore Europe with a self-built van," they say. "Also, that it had to be robust, versatile, and spacious, but narrow enough to drive through villages with small roads. Most important of all was that it had enough headroom to feel comfortable, even on rainy days."

In 2020, they found a vehicle that matched all their criteria: a bright orange Mercedes-Benz Sprinter 313, which they dubbed Orangejuicze. "We fell in love with it immediately, and a year later, after completing our bachelor studies, we converted it in just two months," the skilled duo recounts. "We wanted the interior design to be multifunctional: a perfect vehicle for a full-time vanlife," they say of their aims for the conversion. "In terms of design, we opted for a friendly and open spatial concept. We wanted the bright, minimalist interior to interact with all the beautiful places we would come to discover, so that a ray of sunshine or the interplay of light and shadow could lend their own patterns to the design."

The inside of the Sprinter is, indeed, refined and roomy, enlivened by solid oak countertops, wood and off-white walls, and a thick, cream linen used for the van's rear curtains and seating upholstery. "These elements transform the van into a small apartment," the couple explains. Much of the vehicle's light, meanwhile, comes courtesy of its lengthy windows, which allow Hopfstock and Simon to enjoy the ever-changing landscapes they encounter on their travels. "They're a pretty unique feature," the pair notes.

Their kitchen is similarly special. "We put a lot of emphasis on good food and good company, so we created a kitchen that is spacious with plenty of surface space," they say of the cooking area and remarkably roomy dining zone, replete with long benches to accommodate multiple guests. "The sitting area actually doubles as our full-size bed. It can be transformed in a few simple steps, offering several people room to eat, work, or watch the evening fade to night."

Hopfstock and Simon's favorite feature, however, is the van's rooftop terrace, which they describe as being "perfect for enjoying sunrises, sunsets, and starry

*The vibrant van stops at a viewpoint (opposite).*

Best travel companion *(above left)*. Game break *(above right)*. The breakfast nook on the water *(right)*.

skies." In keeping with the Sprinter's multifunctional interior, the terrace features a solar panel that folds up to serve as a backrest for rooftop visitors.

So far, the pair have traveled to Germany, Switzerland, Italy, Albania, Greece, Macedonia, Montenegro, Bosnia and Herzegovina, Croatia, Slovenia, France, Monaco, and Spain in their eye-catching orange van. "The worst experience we've had so far was getting stuck in a riverbed in Albania," they recount. "Luckily, the locals were able to get us back on the road using an excavator." Happily, this same trip also resulted in Hopfstock and Simon's most memorable vanlife moment to date, when they "parked in a beautiful bay in Albania, directly on the beach, and were woken up by cows the next morning." ∎

## DETAILED VEHICLE INFORMATION

Durable and reliable, with plenty of well-lit open space, Sprinters are a favorite among van conversion specialists with an eye for design. As with other editions, the 313 is named according to weight capacity (three tons) and power (130 h.p.) and boasts a Common Rail Diesel Injection engine. Orangejuicze's expertly converted interior demonstrates the Sprinter's propensity for total transformation: you could be forgiven for mistaking its tasteful, multifunctional design for that of a studio apartment.

| Manufacturer | MERCEDES-BENZ | Year | 2008 |
| --- | --- | --- | --- |
| Model | SPRINTER 313 CDI L2H2 | Mileage | 220,000 KM (136,700 MI) |

The Orangejuicze van blending
in with the locals (above).

# A Country-Chic Peugeot Conversion

When partners Conor Lowndes and Mattie Hanahoe decided to move from Ireland to Italy for work, they seized the opportunity to mark a new chapter with a new van. They sold their previous conversion, and, upon arrival in Milan in late 2020, began scouting out a vehicle to make their own. They soon discovered a 1972 Peugeot J7, a small, characterful front-wheel-drive van in blue and white that ticked all the boxes, and set to work. "We did the entire conversion on the streets of Milan with limited tools and space," the couple reminisces. "We relied on borrowed and gifted tools from generous and interested passersby."

When it came to the van's plumbing and wiring, they wanted to reduce the number of moving parts and electrical components to lessen the chances of malfunction. "For the sink tap we have a mechanical foot pump," they say, "and, for electricity, we opted for large power banks that can be charged with solar panels rather than integrated wiring."

Inspired by their previous conversion, which they had constructed from "mostly free and salvaged materials," this time around they used scrap pallet wood to reimagine the Peugeot's interior as "a simplistic, rugged design." The aim, they say, was to create an indoor space that felt like a beach hut or cabin, something that the pallets, with their "rustic character," easily allowed for. These form the basis for the cabinetry too, which is similarly "country chic," an effect enhanced by the jute rope handles that adorn the drawers and the wicker storage baskets nestled on the kitchen shelves. At the back of the van, larger baskets sit beneath the couple's bed, the frame of which boasts a handy drawer that pulls out to provide an extra countertop for outdoor cooking when the back doors are open. Meanwhile, the upholstery and fabrics that enliven the cozy space consist of warm browns, rust orange, sea green, tan, and cream in keeping with the organic feel of the carpentry.

"The most striking element of our van is its almost panoramic windows," says the duo regarding the Peugeot's huge apertures. "They let in lots of natural light, making wherever the van is parked a big feature in how the interior feels." The build also features a wood-burning stove—"it normally bends a few necks when people see smoke coming from the chimney," they joke. And that's not the only reason the van draws attention. "This model is

Soaking in the sights along the way (opposite).

Coffee with a view (*above left*). Banana pancakes on the road (*above right*). Wood chopping for the day, done (*right*).

uncommon in this part of the world," say Lowndes and Hanahoe. "The old design always intrigues other travelers and frequently sparks conversation."

The van's age and model mean that it travels slowly, and there is no air-conditioning or cruise control installed. But, the partners note, these shortcomings are what make traveling in the Peugeot so unique. "Due to its lack of speed, we resort to taking the back roads, which are always where the best impromptu adventures begin," they say. Since getting their conversion on the road, the couple has explored parts of Italy, Switzerland, Austria, Croatia, Slovenia, and Bosnia and Herzegovina. "Our favorite travel experiences are always when we've parked up somewhere beautiful and remote with a glass of wine and sore bodies from whatever activity we have just finished," they say. "We have had very few bad experiences in the van so far, to be honest, and we certainly don't dwell on any experiences we didn't enjoy." ∎

## DETAILED VEHICLE INFORMATION

Peugeot produced the J7 between 1965 and 1980. This compact front-wheel-drive van features all-around independent suspension, ample cargo space, an easy-to-access engine, and a light, comfortable driver's cabin. J7s are cheaper and roomier than their Volkswagen counterparts, and yet are just as distinctive in their retro aesthetic. The original J7 interior featured a heavy use of plastic, but Lowndes and Hanahoe gave their van a country-cabin-style facelift using scrap pallet wood and other natural materials.

| Manufacturer | PEUGEOT | Year | 1972 |
|---|---|---|---|
| Model | J7 | Mileage | 100,000 KM (62,137 MI) |

Pausing to take in the views (*above*).

# Exploring Rustic Greece on Roads Less Traveled

*For globe-roaming Valeria Pixner and Lukas Unterholzner, when it comes to wintering, there is no place more giving than Greece.*

**Greece** | Sometimes the road less traveled is closer than you think. Valeria Pixner and partner Lukas Unterholzner first fell for vanlife when they explored the United States, Australia, New Zealand, and Patagonia in rented converted vans, but to date, their most cherished trip is the 10 wintry months they spent on the road in Greece. It wasn't, however, the initial choice for their inaugural journey. In springtime 2020, the pair had planned to travel east towards Iran and Mongolia, but the pandemic changed their route: "Over the last few years, we have traveled to many beautiful countries all over the world, but this first winter in Greece is still one of our favorite trips so far," shares Pixner. Their off-road camper is a fully self-sufficient converted 1990 Toyota Hilux LN 105 Double Cab fitted with a bedroom, kitchen, living area, and bathroom, as well as water tanks, a lithium battery, and solar panels. In Greece, they fared superbly: their four-wheel drive and high-ground clearance meant they could easily venture off the beaten track in search of isolated camp spots, their slim profile made it easy to navigate narrow rural roads, and even their winter-proofing came in handy for snow. "Greece is known for its 'warmer' temperatures during winter, but snowfall is not uncommon, even on the beach. On both of our trips to Greece, we witnessed heavy snowfall in the coastal areas. For us, it was no big thing. We're well equipped for snow—we carry snow chains, shovels, and sandboards, and the four-wheel drive helps a lot."

The trip began with a ferry from Ancona, Italy, to Igoumenitsa, one of Greece's largest passenger ports. From this point, they had only a rough sketch of an itinerary to orient them. Their first point of interest was the island Lefkada on the Ionian Sea, just 136 kilometers (84.5 miles) south of their entry port and connected to the mainland by a spindly causeway and floating bridge. On the inland front, they traveled to Meteora—their trip highlight a UNESCO World Heritage List rock formation, with magical 14th-century Orthodox monasteries perched on high cliffs. Last on their list was the popular camping route along the Peloponnese peninsula, which boasts the highest concentration of ancient sites in all of Greece. En route their itinerary, fed by word-of-mouth and happenstance, grew to encompass Evia, Greece's second-largest island after Crete, so close to Athens it appears to be floating just off the coast. In reality, it is linked by two bridges for an easy drive over. During the especially quiet winter, as much of Europe was in lockdown, they found many regions all but deserted. "Most of the time we were completely alone, especially on the islands of Lefkada and Evia, and the Pelion and Chalkidiki regions of the mainland," says Pixner. The pair ended up spending the whole winter exploring, from the dwindling fall of November 2020 to the onset of spring in April 2021. "To be honest, at the beginning it really wasn't planned to stay several months in Greece. But then we just fell in love with the landscape, with the stunning beaches, with the food and the friendly people," shares Pixner.

It was so much so that in November 2021, they decided to spend another winter in Greece, staying until March 2022. "Our second trip to Greece was more planned. Because we fell so deeply in love with the country, we knew that we wanted to see more of it!" says Pixner. This time they knew exactly where they'd begin. "The island of Lefkada was our main highlight on both trips. The landscape and beaches there are just outstanding. And the fact that we were nearly the only campers on the island, especially during our first trip, made it very special for us," explains Pixner. South of Thessaloniki, Chalkidiki is part of the region of Central Macedonia where the couple also discovered pristine beaches, including favorites Kassandra and Sithonia. Next, they headed to the Pelion Peninsula in southeastern Thessaly, which is often referred to as

Driving almost on water, Greece *(opposite).*

NORTH MACEDONIA

ALBANIA

Chalkidiki

Meteora

Igoumenitsa

GREECE

Pelion

Lefkada

Evia

Peloponnese

Enjoying the turquoise
waters *(above)*. Setting up
for a beach sunset *(right)*.

one of Greece's "secret" peninsulas. But the absolute
highlight of the trip was their two and a half months
spent in Crete. As Greece's largest island, its varied
landscape offers abundant adventures. "Crete is just the
perfect island for a long road trip. The beaches are
stunning, there are lovely towns to explore, for example,
Chania, many spectacular gorges to hike through, and
a mountainous landscape with snowcapped mountains
and hidden tiny villages," shares Pixner. Best of all?
After two trips, there's still so much more of Greece
to explore. ∎

Camping on the beach *(top)*.
A radiant Grecian sunset *(above left)*. Off-roading through a canyon *(right)*. One of Greece's dramatically winding coastal roads *(opposite)*.

# A Minibus Motor Home for Better Work and Play

For many, vanlife is funded by necessary periods of time spent stationary, raising the funds for off-grid adventuring. But Australian couple Clare Austin and David Dimech, both licensed physiotherapists, envisioned a clever work-around that benefits both them and their clients. The duo met during their studies at the University of Sydney, and upon graduating, opted to rent a house together just outside of the city. They felt mounting pressure to own their own home, yet were hesitant to commit to large mortgage payments or settling down in one location. Noting that high-quality healthcare is often hard to come by for Australia's rural and remote communities, and tempted by the idea of a more peripatetic lifestyle, they decided to convert a bus into a traveling home and drive around the country to provide just that.

They spent months looking for the perfect vehicle, before settling on a 21-seater, 2007 Toyota Coaster B50, which had previously been used as a community bus. The white minibus arrived in October 2019, and the couple embarked on a year-long mission to transform its interior into their dream dwelling on wheels. Neither Austin nor Dimech had any experience in camper conversions, but that didn't stop them.

Aided by the online community of vanlifers, they gutted the bus's large interior and completed all aspects of the build themselves, except the gas and plumbing. The hardest part, they said, was installing solar panels and an off-grid electrical system—an endeavor that paid off, however, as they now know how to fix any electrical problems that might arise during their travels. They also incorporated a round skylight into the bus's roof, which floods the interior with light, offering a view of the stars from their sleeping area below.

When it came to designing the inside layout, the partners had a few prerequisites: they knew they wanted to include a bathroom with a shower and to install a built-in bed (the idea of having to convert a sofa every day filled them with dread). Now a double bed occupies the rear of the bus, while the rest of the space features an attractive kitchen and living area, made up of orange-hued wood and white paneling. The couple has employed a few nifty hacks to maximize versatility within their small living quarters. A flip-down, rotatable wooden table sits alongside the green-velvet-upholstered seating, providing a surface for work or

*Enjoying endless views from the van's rooftop deck (opposite).*

Australian sunlight *(above left)*. Two Akubra hats hang at the ready *(above right)*. Kangaroo watch *(right)*.

dining, while the extendable kitchen tap can be maneuvered through the window above the sink and used as an outdoor showerhead.

Now, the Toyota feels like a proper apartment, yet allows the couple to operate their business, dubbed Project Physio, while living life on the road. They offer locum physiotherapy services at clinics, hospitals, and aged care units, "or any other clinical setting in need of an extra set of hands," as their website reads, and organize "pop-up" clinics in remote areas. Physically and mentally demanding, physiotherapy is a profession that can quite often lead to burnout among its practitioners. For Austin and Dimech, however—who have so far ventured along Australia's east and south coasts and are currently exploring its western shores—this existence provides plenty of downtime in nature, creating a healthy balance between rewarding work and restorative play. ∎

# DETAILED VEHICLE INFORMATION

The Toyota Coaster is a single-decker minibus, first introduced in 1969. Retired Coasters make for excellent camper conversions: capacious enough to allow for versatile layout options, they are compact enough to drive through national parks or into towns. Austin and Dimech's Coaster is a third-generation model, equipped with a more aerodynamic exterior than its predecessors. They've rendered it the perfect refuge from their busy work lives and can often be found lounging on its wooden roof deck.

| Manufacturer | TOYOTA | Year | 2007 |
|---|---|---|---|
| Model | COASTER B50 | Mileage | 370,000 KM (229,907 MI) |

Gazing upon Uluru
(above).

# The Converted School Bus That Keeps on Dreaming

Three dreams sparked Andi Talbot to build Bodhi, his converted Chevy van made of 90 percent recycled, upcycled, and salvaged materials. "My whole life I'd been wanting to do the ultimate West Coast road trip from Vancouver Island to Cabo San Lucas, months of surfing, sightseeing, and exploring the endless corners of California's coastline that I'd grown up hearing about," explains Talbot. The second dream was to reconnect with Mother Earth and humanity, and to meet open-minded people along the way. Lastly, he wanted to break the seemingly endless cycle of paying rent and needing to pack up and move every other year. Instead, he shares, "I needed a sea turtle shell. So, I followed my intuition and bought a 1990 Chevy van G30 Thomas School Bus the next morning on Craigslist."

True to his intentions, it was not to become just a camping van but a creative meeting space for like-minded travelers. "The end goal was to create a cozy, interactive living space, art studio, and gallery that would draw people in like a West Coast campfire," he says. Talbot poured these sentiments into his work on the van. He worked for nearly five months, through winter storms, for 10 to 15 hours a day. The materiality mattered too: he wanted to showcase the beauty of local wood in the van and "let the natural curves of the red cedar and driftwood flow through the whole project." To do so, he salvaged 95 percent of the wood and metal from friends, mills, and scrapyards, and his dedicated woodworking, largely solo, quickly became a kind of meditation.

Perhaps the most accomplished piece, and definitely the most time consuming, was the floating crystal table, intended to symbolize a tidal pool, built at the "heart" of the van. "I spent weeks digging out rot, sanding, and epoxying until the whole cedar burl was filled with hundreds of crystals, lights, phosphorescents, and beachcombed items from around the world," he says. There are fairy lights, too, that charge up phosphorescent powder so the table glows, as intended, like a West Coast tidal pool. The rest of the interior is equally as focused on wonder and on welcoming. It's designed to be an "open walk-through," the camper-van equivalent of open-plan, and houses handmade quirks like a library reading nook, an elk-antler hat rack, and curved live-edge shelves. And the wonders do not stop

Parking up at the azure, Bahía Concepción, Mexico *(opposite)*.

there: there is red cedar decking, complete with a storage compartment on the top deck, plus wooden scaffolding to hold two hammocks ("the ultimate Baja edition for siestas and checking the surf," according to Talbot). The decking functions as an outdoor living, socializing, and sleeping space. Together, he and Bodhi, have traversed the USA, Canada, and

Mexico. Though it hasn't always been sunshine—he once blew a tire crossing the Mexican border in 50°C (122°F) heat and found himself stranded in the desert. Despite unavoidable bumps in the road, the upside remains the focus for Talbot. His greatest joy along the road? "Connecting with all the kindred beautiful souls around every bend." ∎

## DETAILED VEHICLE INFORMATION

This Chevrolet School Bus was completely overhauled into a home and art space, using repurposed materials such as wood, metal, and found items. In addition to practical features like a kitchenette, the quirky interior contains a communal handmade crystal table, a library reading nook, and live-edge shelving. A surfboard rack adorns the side of the van and on top is a deck built of red cedar wood, complete with a storage compartment and wooden frame for two hammocks.

| Manufacturer | CHEVROLET | Year | 1990 |
|---|---|---|---|
| Model | VAN G30 THOMAS SCHOOL BUS | Mileage | 145,000 KM (90,099 MI) |

A welcoming interior in wood (*above*). Celebrations on the roof terrace (*opposite*).

# A Pumpkin-Colored Kombi to Raise a Smile

"Stella came into our lives back in early 2018," says Mattea Carson of her and her partner Jordan McArthur's pumpkin-colored 1975 Volkswagen T2 Kombi. "We had plans to circumnavigate Australia, and Kombi vans quickly became an obsession of mine." The pair spent months trawling the internet for their ideal VW and stumbled upon Stella. "She was the third bus we had arranged to see and, as she sat there looking pretty in the owner's front yard, we knew she had to be ours," Carson recalls. "Many VW enthusiasts would call her a 'late bay high-light' [because of her bay windshield and elevated headlights], and she is fitted out as a pop-top camper, so is designed to live on the open road."

The van had been recently repainted, with new front seats installed, but the interior was "completely empty," says Carson: "a perfect blank canvas for us to make our own." Never having lived in a van before, but equipped with shrewd eyes for detail thanks to their careers in photography, the duo embarked on designing Stella's interior. "As Kombis aren't the most spacious, we went with a neutral interior to make the space feel bigger," Carson explains of the primarily wood and white-painted decor, warmed by flashes of the same satsuma orange as the van's exterior and the tan-colored canvas of its pop-top roof. White, cream, and pale-grey upholstery, cushion covers, and throws

further contribute to the air of capacious calm. Thanks to Australia's largely warm climate, Carson and McArthur can also count on the outdoors to offer up valuable extra living space most of the time. "To this day, we really love our slide-out drawer," they say of the bench-cum-countertop that sits along the van's side entrance and pulls out to provide surface space for "cooking and hanging out outside the van."

Stella's most unique feature is her color, the couple reflects, while the free-wheeling 1970s nostalgia she evokes renders her a popular sight among fellow travelers. "There aren't too many orange vans cruising on the road these days, especially ones that look so cute!" enthuses Carson. "Stella is 47 years old, and at times, she feels like our very own time machine. She represents an era that was free and full of good vibes. As we travel around, we feel her sharing this energy in each place. We can see by the look on people's faces that she affects them in a positive way." Likewise, Carson's favorite thing about her Kombi is her "sweet smiling face," punctuated by "her headlights and eyelashes," while McArthur enjoys the toy-like nature of her transformative pop-up roof.

**Parked between the palms, under a pastel sky (opposite).**

To date, the pair and Stella have traversed almost every state and territory within Australia. "We have been taking it slow and enjoying the diverse landscapes found in each place," says Carson, adding that next year, they plan to ship Stella over to New Zealand to continue their vanlife forays. "The most difficult time we've had in our van was during the pandemic, when we found ourselves 4,000 kilometers (2,485 miles) from home with no place to go," the couple reveals, adding that their best time happened recently, and completely coincidentally. "By chance, we met up with two other Volkswagen owners from different parts of the country, and for the next week or so, we enjoyed many precious moments as we convoyed across the south coast of Australia." ■

## DETAILED VEHICLE INFORMATION

With its "friendly" face, bright-orange hue, and 1970s aura (even its license plate reads "75 vibes"), this Type 2 Kombi is one of the most cheerful vans around. Carson and McArthur have contrasted Stella's zesty exterior with a minimalist interior that creates the illusion of extra space, while the pop-top roof offers extra height. As Kombis' odometers reset after 99,999 kilometers (62,136 miles), the duo will never know how far Stella has traveled to date, but so far, she has proved a durable and delightful companion.

| Manufacturer | VOLKSWAGEN | Year | 1975 |
| --- | --- | --- | --- |
| Model | T2 KOMBI | Mileage | UNKNOWN |

Breakfast in the pop-up tent bed (*above*). A small companion takes a rest (*opposite*).

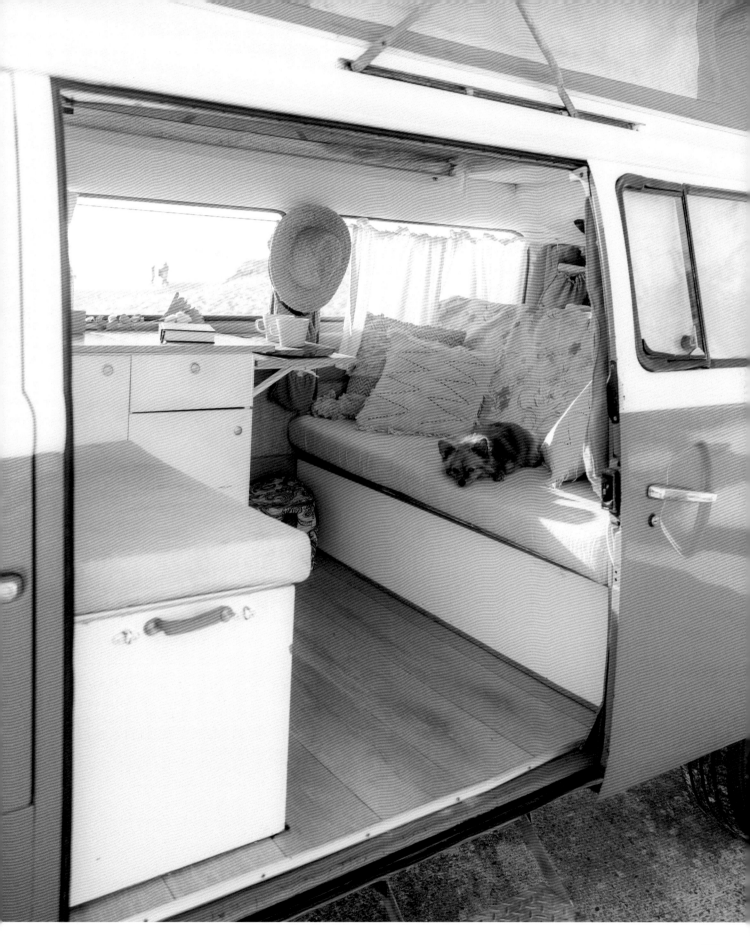

# A Cool Conversion of a Classic

When Ben Quesnel started a new job at Facebook, he decided he needed a side project to keep himself occupied on the weekends. He had also just taken up surfing and, for the first time in his life, required a car. "I connected the dots and thought it would be fun to restore an old van from the ground up," he says.

He bought a 1985 Volkswagen T3 Vanagon GL on Craigslist, which he named Jozette. "She was old and ugly with a broken odometer stuck at 161,557 kilometers (260,000 miles)." Quesnel was a novice when it came to vehicles. All he knew was that he wanted a Volkswagen "because they're cool," with a water-cooled engine "because I'd read that air-cooled engines were slow." Once Jozette was in his possession, however, he set out to learn all there is to know about Vanagons and began scheming the renovation. "I decided to use the same layout VW used in their camper collaboration with Westfalia," he explains. "But I wanted to change certain features and dimensions to better fit my personal needs."

This meant, for instance, creating a narrower bed to allow for more capacious side cabinets, as well as shunning the Volkswagen raisable roof in a bid to allow more light into the van's interior. "I created a ragtop sunroof instead by cutting a one-by-one-meter hole in the roof. That was nerve-racking but it's the upgrade I've enjoyed the most," he explains, adding that the wooden decking above makes for ideal sunset viewing. Another unique element of Quesnel's self-converted camper is its hand-painted exterior. "It was a tired, cracked, deep blue, and I painted it a cheerful yellow with white touches. I built this van in the spirit of its older version, the Kombi, and curated every element to bridge those two design eras [the '50s and the '80s]."

Inside, Quesnel has struck a neat balance between the aesthetically pleasing and the practical. White walls are interspersed with maple cabinets, while the van's sleek countertops are made of pine. The floor is covered by a patterned vinyl, a necessary waterproof solution for a surfer, topped by a woolen Mexican rug for warmth. Separated wooden slats form the headliner, lending the space a boat-like feel, while hidden shelving units create valuable storage space. Out back, Quesnel has installed an outdoor shower and washing-up area attached to a discreetly housed refillable water tank. A small drawer that opens to reveal a pop-out

*The VW winds through the lush Mexican tropics (opposite).*

The van office setup *(opposite)*. Strumming a tune in the afternoon sun *(above left)*. Trinkets from along the way *(above right)*.

dish-drying rack and a carefully tucked-away wooden shower base reveal Quesnel's knack for simple innovation. As does his passenger seat, which boasts a swivel function that allows it to face the van's central seating area in between journeys.

Quesnel and Jozette have traveled far and wide together across the United States, Canada, and Mexico. Quesnel's favorite off-grid adventure occurred when he was driving the infamous Icefields Parkway, a 227-kilometer (172-mile) road that connects Jasper and Banff National Parks in Alberta. "I stopped for the night in front of the Athabasca Glacier, and as I stepped out of the van at sunset, a fox silently approached me," he recalls. "His curiosity exceeded his fear, and we hung out together for many long minutes in silence." Quesnel's worst moment occurred when Jozette's engine overheated while ascending a mountain in Queretaro, Mexico. "Thankfully, it turned out my radiator fan's fuse had blown so I was able to change it, let the engine cool down, and keep going." There's no doubt that Quesnel and Jozette can rise to the challenges of the road. ■

## DETAILED VEHICLE INFORMATION

A third iteration of the Volkswagen Type 2, the 1985 van was marketed with different names around the world—the Transporter and Caravelle in continental Europe, T25 in the UK, Microbus in South Africa, and in North and South America as Vanagon (a portmanteau that implies it drives as smoothly as a station wagon but is as roomy as a van). Jozette is a camper conversion with a unique colorway, a moveable sunroof, and a bespoke take on the traditional Volkswagen van layout. Additional details include an outdoor shower and washing-up area, a sleek side awning, and a roof terrace for sunset watching.

| Manu-facturer | VOLKSWAGEN | Year | 1985 |
|---|---|---|---|
| Model | T3 VANAGON GL | Mileage | 483,000 KM (300,000 MI) |

# The Highs and Lows of Bolivia's Altiplano

*Shruthi and Peter Lapp headed to Bolivia to undertake the country's breathtaking—and challenging—Lagunas Route through the Andean High Plateau.*

**Bolivia** | Couple Shruthi and Peter Lapp traded city life in the USA for everyday adventure on the wide-open road. During a longer trip through South America, Bolivia was high on their list. "Bolivia seemed like such an otherworldly place, and it didn't feel right to drive to the end of the South American continent without visiting it," they explain. The pair planned their trip around two must-see destinations in the high altitudes of southwest Bolivia, the Salar de Uyuni, the world's largest salt flat, and the Lagunas Route, which stretches across the Andes High Plateau down to Chile.

"Since this was part of a longer journey, we had no strict time limit or itinerary to stick to. We did basic research about both excursions online to see the route itself and gauge how much gas and other provisions we'd need to stock up on," the couple says. "Besides that, the plan was to explore these beautiful places and take it day by day."

The Bolivian Altiplano, though stunning, can be a hostile area, especially in the arid southwest, in contrast to more humid climes in the lower eastern country. The Lapps came duly equipped for colder weather than at sea level: "The only preparations we had for Bolivia's climate were plenty of warm layers, sleeping bags, down feather comforter, and a propane heater we brought with us from the United States."

Their travel essentials for the salt flats include sunscreen, moisturizer, and sunglasses to counteract the strength of the reflective sun and dry climate. And, crucially, old-school maps. "There are many stretches in Bolivia where human contact or a cell signal are hard to find. We highly recommend finding an up-to-date paper map as a backup to any offline maps you may have saved on your phone," they explain.

The pair traversed the challenging terrain in their trusty 1987 Volkswagen T3 Vanagon GL Westfalia, their permanent home on the road. "The great thing about the van is that it still functions as a home even if we have to be stationary due to any inevitable issues you'd have with a vehicle that's over 30 years old," they say. "It already had the necessary preparations for driving South American terrain: bigger shocks, lift springs, bigger tires, limited-slip differential."

There were, however, some unexpected bumps in the road. "There were many surprises along the way! Neither of us was prepared for just how wild and rugged this part of Bolivia was going to be," share the Lapps. Their trusty Volkswagen didn't always take to the high altitudes, and one day, it just wouldn't start. "We were above 4,500 meters (14,764 feet) and our hope was that getting down to lower altitude would allow the van to warm up enough to start. Our plan worked, and the van started up as usual as soon as we got down lower!" Luckily, they had set out on the journey in a convoy of friends who were able to tow them. "This route can be really isolated in many places, and we were really happy about our decision to drive this route with friends. We highly recommend this just in case the unexpected happens!"

Then, there was the issue of repeated water exposure. "We kept having a recurring electrical issue due to water from the salt flat spraying under the van," the couple explains. "Our engine is in the rear and fairly exposed to the elements, so it's necessary to use caution and limit water crossings as much as possible. Large portions of the salt flat were covered in water, which was unavoidable and ultimately resulted in the van randomly losing power."

The high altitudes, however, have high payoffs, including the surreal optical illusions of the salt flats and their attendant flocks of flamingos. "The highlight of the trip was the experience of driving on the salar [salt flats]. It was unlike anything we had done before, because we were driving and camping on the largest salt desert in the world," they share. "We will never forget the feeling of driving into what felt like an infinite landscape, barely seeing any

Sighting flamingos high up on the Bolivian Altiplano (opposite).

CHILE

Salar de Uyuni

BOLIVIA

Uyuni

Laguna Pastos Grandes

Laguna Capina

Laguna Colorada

Laguna Blanca

San Pedro de Atacama

ARGENTINA

**Warming up with the last of the day's sun *(above)*. Stretching out to read in the front seats *(right)*.**

other people for days, or the panoramic views during sunset."

Along the road and in and around their quick-thinking problem solving, the two found a peaceful routine in their changing everyday life. "A typical day included getting out of bed when the sun warmed up the inside of the van, enjoying sunshine, some coffee, breakfast, and driving," explain the Lapps. "We would try to cover as much ground as possible, with stops to explore anything that looked interesting on foot. We chose our adventures based on how we felt that day. At the end of the day, we would settle down into a camp spot, make something warm to drink, and have happy hour while watching the sunset. It was such a simple but delightful routine." ■

Grazing goats *(top)*.
The cozy sleeping quarters
*(bottom left)*. Lapp beneath
a palm *(bottom right)*.
The Laguna Colorada,
Bolivia *(opposite)*.

# A New Life Off the Grid

Sometimes, all it takes to change the course of your life is an impulse buy and a passing conversation. At least, so it went for filmmaker and photographer Kai Branss: "I found this bus by accident together with my girlfriend. We saw it and bought it the next day," he says of his now-converted school bus. Then, there was a chance conversation in a Portuguese laundromat, sometime later with a fellow traveler, who'd spent 10 years out on the road. "While waiting for our laundry to finish, we were talking and he said, 'You really need to be very careful with this life because you won't be able to go back.' Several months later, on my way back to Germany, I knew he was right and moved out of my apartment," shares Branss. The initial plan had simply been to take the 1993 Vandura School Bus out for climbing trips and stay up in the mountains. To do so, Branss and his girlfriend started building out the van: "We stripped down the bus completely and started with a blank canvas. That was a challenge, but also very rewarding to build something with your own hands," says Branss, who taught himself the tricks of the trade by watching YouTube tutorials.

To stay out in the wild for longer periods, the bus needed to be fully off the grid. In order to be able to work remotely, sufficient power was critical for Branss, who kitted the van out with enough charge for all-day laptop work and charging equipment. Then came water: in order to be as environmentally friendly and plastic-free as possible, he installed a filtration system, which allows him to draw from lakes, rivers, fountains, or taps at gas stations, and store the water in four 25-liter canisters, that, in total, can last him up to a week. But for all its convenient facilities, the bus has a rather inconvenient habit of breaking down often. "I spend quite some time living in a workshop waiting for spare parts to arrive and getting the bus fixed," says Branss. "I can do a lot by myself but there are just some things that you need a proper workshop for. It's pretty difficult to find a good mechanic in Europe that is up for working on a U.S. school bus. The best places for that are Greece and Portugal, and I even found a great guy on the Canary Islands," he adds. To ease the waiting game and give him more flexibility, Branss recently added a bike deck to tow along his XT250 Yamaha Motorcycle. "Still being mobile when your house can't move anymore is a huge plus and a real lifesaver," he says.

The former school bus on a seaside route (opposite).

Firing up the woodstove
*(above left)*. The cozy wooden
interior *(above right)*.
Preparing food in the great
outdoors *(right)*.

By now, whether on bike or bus, he's traveled
through Austria, Italy, France, Corsica, the Canary
Islands, Greece, Spain, Croatia, England, Belgium, the
Netherlands, Poland, the Czech Republic, Switzerland,
and Andorra. "After some smaller trips, I fell in love with
this lifestyle so much that the times in the apartment
got shorter and shorter because I wanted to stay in the
bus longer and longer," he admits. Like many before
him, he was drawn to the minimalist but brimful life
on the road, carrying very few possessions, rising with
the sun and sleeping after nightfall. It was so much so
that he moved out of his apartment and into the van
full-time. "My favorite part of vanlife is the ever-changing
front yard and being so exposed to the elements and
nature. The wind, rain, the sounds you hear at night in
a forest, the crackling fire of my woodstove. I love
the simplicity of this lifestyle, the ability to go wherever
I want to, and being able to stay as long as I want to.
That option is priceless." ∎

## DETAILED VEHICLE INFORMATION

To ready the former school bus for the road, the vehicle was completely stripped and rebuilt for off-grid living. A water filtration system means water can be drawn from any source and tanks onboard can hold up to 100 liters (26.4 gallons). The van supplies sufficient power for a laptop workstation, plus extra charge for equipment. Inside, it includes the perk of a composting toilet. A bike deck on the exterior means an XT250 Yamaha Motorcycle is often along for the ride.

| Manufacturer | THOMAS BUILT BUSES | Year | 1993 |
| --- | --- | --- | --- |
| Model | GMC VANDURA G3500 | Mileage | 250,000 KM (155,342 MI) |

Out on the open road
(above).

# A Four-by-Four Fitted with Vanlife Comforts

In the throes of the Covid-19 pandemic, as the threat of lockdown loomed over his hometown of Sydney, Australia, Oliver Dykes decided it was time to buy himself some freedom, or a 2004 Land Rover Defender 110 TD5 to be exact. The three-door wagon was a former army vehicle and is a rare sight in Australia. "Land Rover only ever sold the 110 TD5 as a five-door here," explains Dykes. "The Australian army imported this model for a small test program."

The truck was delivered from Queensland to Sydney "looking a lot like a military truck in full camo," Dykes recalls. As Sydney finally went into lockdown, Dykes and his partner Jade Peace took the opportunity to convert it into a camper. "I set myself a brief to build a modern classic and proceeded to tear down the whole thing in our rental apartment's shared garage in Sydney," says Dykes. The renovation took nine months in total and involved "stripping, sanding, repair work, reconditioning, upholstering, painting, and galvanizing," he describes—tasks he undertook himself, with assistance from Peace and friends. "The engine has stayed relatively standard, with a few upgrades for the Australian climate, but every bolt, hinge, rubber, and seal has been replaced on the body."

Dykes and Peace opted to paint the wagon's exterior a warm shade of yellow, lending the vehicle its nickname, SunnySideUp. They had a Mulgo pop-top roof installed to create extra height and their principal sleeping space. "It's what enables us to live and work in the truck full-time, allowing us to stand up and move around," they say—something that makes the vehicle particularly unique. "It's a four-by-four with all the capabilities that that allows, but has the livability of a van."

The couple designed and fitted all other elements of the interior themselves, including the water system and 12-volt electricity. They made custom cabinetry in rich, orange-toned wood, and created a homey kitchen and living space replete with a covetable sofa in terracotta-colored corduroy. "That's my favorite feature," says Peace. "We can turn it into a daybed for guests, or curl up with a movie or a good book on a rainy day." Dykes, meanwhile, most appreciates SunnySideUp's cheerful paint job. "The color makes me smile every time I see it," he says. "I think my brief worked out quite well, because the first question I get asked about the truck is, 'What year is it?' People always guess the '70s or '80s

*SunnySideUp maneuvers wild off-road conditions (opposite).*

A pop-top bedroom leaves
space below for living
*(opposite)*. A misty beach stop
*(above left)*. The cozy space
up front *(above right)*.

and are surprised to hear
it's a 2004 model with
aircon, power steering,
and Apple CarPlay!"

Dykes and Peace have lived and traveled in
SunnySideUp non-stop for the past 12 months, hiking,
surfing, and reveling in the chance to "explore isolated
and remote areas of Australia independently." They've
encountered a couple of hairy moments along the
way—"once, we almost lost SunnySideUp to the tide
as we raced the ocean to get back to our camp, and
another time to some deceptively soft sand dunes"—but
for the most part have enjoyed only good times in
their truck-turned-tiny-home. "One of the best trips was
completing the 'Old Telegraph Track' to Pajinka in
North Queensland," they recall. "It's 350 kilometers
(217 miles) of rough off-roading, with tricky obstacles
and 14 river crossings, some of them known to have
crocodiles, but it passes through some of the most
beautiful and magical countryside we have had the
privilege to experience. We barely saw another
human and no crocodiles!" ∎

## DETAILED VEHICLE INFORMATION

The Land Rover Defender series comprises a variety
of off-road vehicles, known for their toughness
and versatility. Production began in 1983 with the Land
Rover 110, a name denoting the truck's 110-inch-long
wheelbase. SunnySideUp is a 2004 four-by-four model
and features a TD5 diesel engine. A former army
truck, its nine-seater interior allowed plenty of room
for conversion—especially with the added pop-top
roof. Above this sits an original army-built roof rack,
perfect for surfboard storage.

| Manu-facturer | LAND ROVER | Year | 2004 |
|---|---|---|---|
| Model | DEFENDER 110 TD5 | Mileage | 130,000 KM (80,778 MI) |

# A Remarkably Rustic Ford Transit Turned Shack

When it comes to awe-inspiring van conversions, German vanlifer Piet Weihe's transformation of a 2010 Ford Transit MWB into a decorative cabin is hard to beat. "I just wanted a cozy layout," he says modestly of the inspiration behind his design, defined as it is by intricate woodwork, ornamental glass, and a glorious wood-burning stove. "The first time I saw a fireplace in a van was in New Zealand," he recalls. "At that point, I had been living in a station wagon for about a year, and it made me realize that I needed a bit of an upgrade for my next adventure in Australia."

Upon his arrival in Australia, he began working in a vineyard, saving up the funds for both his van and the fireplace. Once both had been purchased, the vineyard proved the perfect setting to convert the van into the "little wooden cabin on wheels" he had in mind—not only because of the space it offered, but because of the abundance of wooden pallets and wood chips available on-site. "During the building process, I found out about my passion for working with wood," he says, "so I took my time and played around with different patterns." These adorn the deceptively roomy cargo van's walls and cabinetry, and range from parquet to marquetry spanning various shades of brown.

"I also wanted to use local materials, so I went to a nearby timber yard to buy a jarrah slab to create a nice-looking countertop," says Weihe of another of the van's standout details. "It is quite heavy though and splits easily, so it's not the best material to use in a van. I liked that it was red, however, and native to Australia, so I used epoxy to fill in the gaps." Other unique elements include the stained-glass window that separates the driver's cabin from the living space. "I got that from a local lady; I thought it would add some charm and really make the van complete," Weihe explains.

Indeed, it is the combined warming qualities of the colored glass and crackling fire that, for Weihe, have most made his van feel like home. "As I spend a lot of time in the ocean, I wanted to create a cozy environment for when I come inside, especially on cold and rainy days. And there is nothing better than having a glass of wine in the evening with a little fire burning right next to me," he says. A comfortable bed was another top priority. "It's probably the most important part of the van build," says Weihe, "because it's the place where you spend the most time." As such, he was tempted to install

The "Shack on Wheels" parked cliffside above crashing waves, Australia (opposite).

The interior of the van
is inspired by wooden cabins
*(opposite)*. Observing the
ocean from the rooftop deck
*(above left)*. The interior
features Australian jarrah
wood *(above right)*.

a fixed bed, but ended up opting for a "sofa bed on
heavy-duty runners" to allow for more space.

   Now, Weihe has his dream "shack on wheels" to
accompany him on his adventures, and so far, their
worst experience has also proved their best. "Last year
I broke down in the outback of Australia," he recalls. "I'd
been driving down a gravel road for about 160 kilometers
(99 miles) and broke my wheel bearings. I ended up in
a roadhouse where I spent two weeks waiting for the spare
parts and fixing the van up with the help of the people
there. I also made a couple of friends who traveled with
me afterward. In the roadhouse, there was a Murphy's
Law sign saying, 'Anything that can happen, will happen,'
which made me laugh." ∎

## DETAILED VEHICLE INFORMATION

Affordable, dependable, surprisingly spacious and
versatile, Ford Transit vans make for particularly
popular camper bases. Nevertheless, few vanlifers
have realized a metamorphosis as complete as that
of Weihe's rustic shack. Putting in around 850 hours
of work, he transformed an austere cargo van
into an ambient cabin-like dwelling with a warming
wood-burning stove at its heart, a full-sized tiled
shower, and the most exquisitely ornate woodwork,
all carried out by hand.

| Manu-facturer | FORD | Year | 2010 |
|---|---|---|---|
| Model | TRANSIT MWB | Mileage | 560,000 KM (347,968 MI) |

# In Search of Sand Dunes and Ruins in Tunisia

*Gefa Berst and Lukas Reusch headed to Tunisia with dreams of kitesurfing coastlines and off-roading into the Sahara's remote dunes.*

**Tunisia** | As 2021 drew to a close, Gefa Berst and Lukas Reusch headed south to balmy North Africa. "Our travels are fueled on one hand by kitesurfing but also a thirst for adventure," explains Berst. Both digital nomads can work from anywhere, and for a warmer beginning to 2022, Tunisia was at the top of their list, with enough coast to satisfy their passion for kitesurfing and plenty of desert interior for off-road adventures. "We decided to travel to Tunisia in the 'coldest months.' Every day it was around 20 °C (67 °F), sometimes more, sometimes less," says Berst.

When the pair first arrived in northern Tunisia by ferry from Italy, their sights were set south on the Sahara. Here, they experienced the first of many highlights on solitary off-roading adventures in the desert, before continuing their journey, stopping in the desert town of Douz with its vibrant, weekly markets, and visiting the oasis of Ksar Ghilane, home to the ancient Berber village Chenini and its restorative hot springs.

The former tipper truck, a converted Mercedes-Benz 1824 AK, was the perfect steed for Tunisia, impressively equipped for the most challenging of terrain and off-grid living. "We've been converting our vehicle for the last two years exactly for this purpose, to be self-sufficient for several days in remote areas far away from any roads and infrastructure," says Berst. The four-wheel drive is fitted with large tires for high ground clearance, and its competence continues to amaze its owners. In their case, the desert was no feat to traverse: they describe the Sahara's dunes as "butter soft" under their tires. They were, however, always prepared for any eventuality. Their extensive packing list included sand plates, a shovel, jacks, and towing ropes, as well as spare parts. "For emergencies, in case we get stuck, which was the case once in Tunisia, we have all kinds of salvage material with us," says Berst. When they did break down, local generosity meant they were never short of helping hands.

From the arid south, the pair then headed west to the salt lake Chott el Jerid, this time to oases of another kind: the Midès mountain oasis, surrounded by jagged canyons, and the Chebika Oasis, a former Roman outpost and mountain refuge of the Berber people. If you're a Star Wars fan, Berst recommends a visit: the area was the setting of the desert planet Tatooine in the cult films. Last on their western expedition was the vast Chott el Jerid salt lake, the largest in the Sahara.

"Now the east was calling, with all its endless gorgeous sandy beaches," explains Berst. Djerba became their base, and they camped up on the beach with a prime kitesurfing spot right at their doorstep. But the location offered much more than the beach alone. Here, they visited a traditional hammam, sought carpets and ceramics in the souk, and found their favorite Tunisian dish, mechouia salad, a piquant mixture of grilled vegetables including tomatoes, peppers, onions, and garlic. The Djerba area is both an avian paradise (aptly named Flamingo Peninsula) and a street-art hot spot with its vibrant Djerbahood. "Over 300 works of art by international artists adorn the walls of the neighborhood. It's very impressive," says Berst.

For their closing stretch, Berst and Reusch headed north again, this time through the cities of Sfax, Hammamet, and Tunis, where they continued to experience new sides of the country. "Tunis is, in some corners, the complete contrast to all of Tunisia. Everything is modern, good infrastructure, large malls, chic houses," says Berst. "In the north, it becomes greener with vineyards and olive groves." They wisely stocked up on good wine and olive oil before heading home, again via Italy, but not before exploring Roman cultural sites, including UNESCO World Heritage Sites Dougga (also known as Thugga), the best-preserved Roman city in Tunisia, and El Djem with its oval amphitheater.

Out in the remote Tunisian Sahara *(opposite).*

ALGERIA

Tunis

Hammamet

TUNISIA

Sfax

Midès

Chebika Oasis

Chott el Jerid

Douz

Ksar Ghilane

Djerba

Off-roading on the sand
dunes *(above)*. The sleek
kitchen interior *(right)*.

But their lasting memory remains of the people.
"We never thought we would like Tunisia so much,
especially with the camper. We never had any problems.
If we were not too far in the middle of nowhere,
the Tunisian National Guard came every evening to
see if we were okay," says Berst. "We received
a warm welcome here and are so incredibly grateful
that we were allowed to travel to Tunisia. We will
definitely be back!" ■

A motorcycle in tow for the ride *(top)*. Cairns in the desert *(above)*. The former tipper truck is ready for off-roading *(right)*. A sweeping view of the Tunisian desertscape *(opposite)*.

# From Radio-Command Truck to Boho Home

In 2018, German couple Jenni Ball and Flo Ball-Schmid purchased a former radio-command, civil-protection truck from Wilhelmshaven, Lower Saxony, via an online auction. A quirky Mercedes-Benz 307 D model from 1987, the van's exterior is a vibrant orange, something the pair says renders it particularly unusual. "If we've been informed correctly, there were just 30 orange vans of this type built back then," they say. Over the course of just three weekends, the skilled duo, who were then based in Bavaria, converted its interior from "a dreary government space" into "a cozy home on wheels."

They dubbed the distinctly retro tangerine van Dicki (or "thick"), owing to its rather square, squat appearance. "It is really boxy, so we don't lose much space inside," they explain—something, they note, that made fitting furniture, like their pull-out double bed, antique cupboard, and homey kitchen chest of drawers, much easier. "We love a boho vibe," they say of the interior design, "and light, bright colors combined with some Moroccan influences"—and a glance around the inside reveals an array of Moroccan ceramics, including kitchen tiles, as well as decorative string lights.

Initial upgrade complete, the couple spent "every weekend and vacation exploring Europe" in their DIY camper. By 2020, they had come to realize that all they really required in life was "the two of us, our van, and the open road," and without further ado, they left their apartment, quit their jobs, sold most of their possessions, and moved into Dicki full-time. "Our plan was to travel the hippie trail overland to India, so we installed some fittings, built more storage, bought a second stove, and created a rooftop terrace," they say.

Hampered by Covid-19 restrictions, however, they spent much of the year traveling around Europe instead, eventually stopping for the winter in Greece. Adventures in Central and North America ensued the following year, and Dicki was left behind in Germany for a spell, only to incur water damage while Ball and Ball-Schmid were away. After another round of repairs, and the installation of a new battery and solar paneling, they were back on the road, heading first for Scandinavia and the Baltics, then for Georgia and Armenia before venturing to Turkey and Iran, where they are currently located.

*The former radio-command truck with adventure gear in tow (opposite).*

Luminous golden hour
(opposite). The boho-inspired
interior (above left). Cooking
outdoors (above right).

## DETAILED VEHICLE INFORMATION

The Mercedes-Benz 307 D belongs to the T1 (or
Transporter Neu) series, produced between
1977–1995 in Bremen, Germany. Notably larger than
the Volkswagen Transporter, the truck has long
been championed as a first-rate camper conversion
base. Ball and Ball-Schmid have made great use
of their former radio-control truck, embellishing its
4.5-square-meter (48-square-foot) interior with
vintage furnishings, adding a large wooden roof deck
for relaxation and added storage, and a hefty bike
rack to its boxy, eye-popping exterior.

So far, the couple has found Dicki the perfect
road trip companion. "Our favorite thing about the van
is its size," they say. "Of course, when it's raining or
in wintertime, we often wish we had a bigger one, but
for traveling, it is simply the perfect size—especially
on narrow roads or in busy cities. And it's awesome that
it is small enough to fit in normal parking lots." During
the many months they've spent on the road, Ball and
Ball-Schmid have endured their fair share of
tribulations, from vandalism to break-in attempts, but,
for the most part, they are loving their life off-grid.
"We wake up in gorgeous landscapes, meet amazing
people all along the way, and travel with our bed,
our kitchen, our safe space with us. We are free to roam
the world, and that's the best experience ever." ■

| Manu-facturer | MERCEDES-BENZ | Year | 1987 |
|---|---|---|---|
| Model | 307 D | Mileage | 130,000 KM (80,778 MI) |

# Off-Road Living in a Former Deutsche Post Van

In 2015, couple Franziska and Malte Hedrich purchased a 1981 Mercedes L 508 D, known colloquially in Germany as a "Düdo" because they were originally made in Düsseldorf. In its former life, the van had been used by Deutsche Post as a delivery vehicle, but the pair had big dreams to take it on its longest mission yet: crossing continents to reach Singapore. To make the van suit their needs, the Hedrichs embarked on a huge restoration project. Their vehicle was, in fact, the shortest Düdo in length, which, though advantageous for driving narrow streets and maneuvering tight corners, required some invention to make it livable on the inside. Plus, they wanted to go off-road. "We wanted a design especially suitable for off-road tracks, even though it only has two-wheel drive, which is why ground clearance and big tires were important."

The van was stripped to its shell. They cut off the roof and built a higher-pitched roof on top, which, combined with their raising of the vehicle's chassis, brought the van up to 3.2 meters (10.5 feet) high. According to the couple, it's so spacious inside that the tallest of people can stand upright comfortably—which, in van living, is a real novelty. Then, they changed the engine and the axles, switched the back tires from double to single (to make it more suitable for off-road tracks), welded rusty patches, and sanded, smoothed, and painted the entire van themselves. Next, they turned their attention to fitting out the interior, where they made the most of the narrow space and newly added height. The roof cavity now houses a foldable bed, while in the main area there is space to relax, work, cook, or read in the large seating area, complete with two benches and a large table. For long journeys, there are abundant amenities: water tanks that store up to 130 liters (34 gallons), a water filter to make any water potable, solar panels with a capacity of 250 watts, a fridge, a water boiler, a diesel parking heater, an outdoor shower with warm water, Wi-Fi booster antennas, off-road sand ladders, strong lights on the exterior, and ample storage. Beyond the novelty of their off-road Düdo, the owners' list of favorite features goes on: a flash-light bar installed at the front of the van, the crafty sand ladders on the outdoor-kitchen side of the van, and the geometric elephant they painted on the other.

So far, the adventures in their Düdo have been plentiful. "One of the most lasting and impressive

**Camouflaged in the desert (opposite).**

experiences was driving into the foothills of the Sahara, and spending the nights there under millions of stars and in absolute silence," they share. But on the other hand, close calls include sparks coming out of the exhaust in the Italian mountains, to terrifying mudslides in Albania. "There were no cars or anybody passing by—we didn't have a phone or internet connection, and no food!" they say. Thankfully, they navigated their way through the situation. But what about their starting goal of reaching Singapore? Though they haven't quite made it that far yet, they've ticked off a long list of destinations, including Italy, Albania, Turkey, Bulgaria, Romania, Hungary, the Czech Republic, France, Portugal, and Spain. And, the couple concedes, Singapore may still be in the cards one day. ∎

## DETAILED VEHICLE INFORMATION

To make the two-wheel-drive van suitable for off-roading, the owners increased the ground clearance by raising the chassis and switching the back tires from smaller, double ones to larger, single tires. Inside, the roof pitch was raised, and a foldable bed was installed up high. It now boasts facilities that include a water filtration system, a 130-liter (34-gallon) water tank, solar panels with a capacity of 250 watts, a fridge, a water boiler, an outdoor shower, Wi-Fi booster antennas, off-road sand ladders, and plenty of storage.

| Manufacturer | MERCEDES-BENZ | Year | 1981 |
|---|---|---|---|
| Model | L 508 D | Mileage | 236,000 KM (146,644 MI) |

Happy hour with friends after a day on the road (above). Shoveling sand in the Sahara, Tunisia (opposite).

266

# A Family's Journey to Cross the World

Since 2016, an Austrian family—Leander Nardin, Maria Zehentner, and their son Lennox—have been ambitiously crossing the world in their converted truck and permanent family home, Akela. In their first three years alone, they have managed to traverse three continents, from Austria to Australia, totaling 80,000 kilometers (49,710 miles). "We were dissatisfied with the idea of continuing to live as we had for the next few years. We no longer wanted to work for others to finance our lives. We created our own path, trying to become more responsible and self-determined on our own," they explain. "There were several specific goals. At the top was to show our son Lennox the world. We wanted him to see the beauty of this planet with his own eyes. We wanted to give him and ourselves new perspectives and get to know each other as a family."

Their truck of choice was originally a German military vehicle used for border patrol. "It took two years before we were reasonably satisfied and finished with the conversion. Although it was originally designed as a vehicle to protect borders, today it has become a family home to cross them with." The family completely overhauled the military-green vehicle, fitting it with a cabin to provide 12 square meters (129 square feet) of living space and painting the front an eye-catching, deep-turquoise blue. The detailed conversion transformed the vehicle into a completely off-grid home. Akela is fitted with a fully functioning kitchen, complete with a fridge and oven, a water filter, an electronic heater, plus an additional Hobbit wood-burning stove, toilet, shower, and water boiler, as well as high-voltage batteries. "The room layout turned out quite well. Lennox has a cozy nest in the back where he can retreat. The kitchen is big enough to let off steam, and our bedroom above the roof is bigger than you'd think. We feel very comfortable in the small space and don't find ourselves missing anything. Except maybe the occasional hot tub," they joke.

Akela traversing verdant mountain valleys in Wyoming, USA (opposite).

Structurally, they relied on cozy-feeling wood inside, taking inspiration from Austrian alpine huts. "We are a family that likes to be outdoors, so it was important to us to work with natural materials," they explain. "We used several different types of wood in the interior. Among other things, there's a real maple tree trunk that Lennox uses as a ladder to his bed."

The streamlined kitchen leads to Lennox's bed nook *(opposite)*. Lennox takes in Australia's dusty Outback *(above left)*. The trusty woodstove *(above right)*.

Of all the truck's fit-out, it's the wood-burning stove that is the most cherished. "An absolute favorite feature is our woodstove in the front of the seating area. Visually, of course, it emphasizes the ambiance of the rustic hut, but it also serves as a backup in the winter. In Siberia, at -30 °C (-22 °F), our heating stopped working. In situations like this, the stove can save lives." After years of travel, when it comes to their favorite destinations, it's hard to settle on one. "Greece's Meteora monasteries in the rocks were seriously impressive; in Cappadocia in Turkey you think you're in a fairy tale; or along the old Silk Road over the Pamir Highway, one of the highest highways in the world. Then there's traveling 4,000 kilometers (2,485 miles) through Siberia, skiing in Japan, diving in Indonesia, seeing Uluru in Australia, or the Grand Canyon in America," they rattle off. The family is currently based in Canada and shows no signs of slowing down.

"When you drive a truck around the world for five years, there are no best or worse situations. Basically, the truck has given us a life to gain incredible experiences all over the world, from both sides." ∎

## DETAILED VEHICLE INFORMATION

This former military truck has been completely overhauled to function as a full-time roving home. It has been fitted with a cabin that provides 12 square meters (129 square feet) for its three inhabitants, including a raised bedroom area, sizable kitchen with a stovetop, oven, and fridge, sanitary amenities including a bathroom and shower, plus a water boiler and filter. There are two forms of heating, one electronic and the other a wood-burning stove. The truck's amenities are powered by high-voltage batteries, allowing it to operate off-grid as needed.

| Manu- facturer | MERCEDES- BENZ | Year | 1977 |
|---|---|---|---|
| Model | LA 911 B | Mileage | 200,000 KM (124,274 MI) |

# A Simple Yet Striking Kombi Conversion

Meredith Schofield and Sean Brokenshire purchased their Volkswagen T2 Kombi, Etta, in 2015 from a retired policeman who had "bought her as a barn find and restored her back to life." The white and sunflower-yellow van hails from Wolfsburg in Germany, the Australian couple explains, and "was shipped to Australia in pieces in the 1970s and lovingly put together by the hard-working factory hands of Volkswagen Australia in Clayton, Victoria."

Once the Kombi was in their possession, they set to work converting the eight-seater into a van for camping and exploring. "We designed the new interior in such a way that everything inside could be removed with ease and converted back into a traditional microbus if needed," the pair says of the process. "We use Etta for everything, not just camping—she's our daily drive—so we kept the design very simple to save on space and weight."

They removed just one row of seats from the bus and replaced the back seat with a rock and roll bed for sleeping. "We only have what we need and nothing else," they say of the minimalist interior renovation. "We put in a false floor, some basic cabinetry, a stow-away table, and a bench seat that doubles as a storage unit. Then we installed a second battery and a travel fridge that sits perfectly between the two front seats and acts as a great platform for our dog, Bandit." Their favorite thing about their camper, however, is its many windows (eight total), which offer a 360-degree outlook of their shifting surroundings. "Driving down the highway, you can look all around you and soak in the view unobstructed."

As with many older Volkswagens, Etta is a slow and steady travel companion who garners much attention. "In a sea of white converted modern vans, people always get a kick out of seeing Etta on the road, especially heading down a four-wheel-drive track in the middle of nowhere," recounts the pair fondly. "Her color and design are iconic and represent a time when life was more carefree," they observe of the Kombi's countercultural connotations. "She's a symbol of great design and of life on the road."

Despite her considerable age, Schofield and Brokenshire have taken Etta on multiple long-haul, off-the-grid excursions in Australia. "We've traveled over 80,467 kilometers (50,000 miles) together, and as Kombi odometers clock back over to zero once you reach 99,999, we will never know how many miles she's

Taking Bandit the dog out into the surf *(opposite)*.

traveled in her 50 years." As their affectionate descriptions attest, the duo sees Etta as more than just a vehicle. "She has her own personality; it's almost like we are traveling with another person." As such, they are hesitant to reveal any "worst moments" they've had together, besides a few breakdowns—"but we know enough about her engine to get out of most situations"—and a hairy moment involving a large beachside pothole that made the roof rack collapse.

Uplifting memories, on the other hand, abound. "By far the best experience we've had with Etta was traveling around Australia in 2019," the couple recalls. "We traveled over 22,000 kilometers (13,670 miles) from the east coast to the west, before venturing north into the wild and returning home. She was an absolute dream and never faltered—even on corrugated roads, water crossings, and soft sand beaches." ∎

## DETAILED VEHICLE INFORMATION

With their cheerful, retro appearance and associations with long-haul adventuring, early Volkswagen Kombis remain a firm favorite among aesthetically inclined bus owners. Their roomy interiors and removable seats render them ripe for conversion and, once equipped with the basics for sleeping and living, they can easily be switched from family-size minibus to van and back. "That's what is so great about owning a Kombi," say Schofield and Brokenshire. "They're so adaptable to whatever you need."

| Manufacturer | VOLKSWAGEN | Year | 1975 |
|---|---|---|---|
| Model | T2 KOMBI | Mileage | UNKNOWN |

Blending into the desertscape (*above*). The best pal along the road (*opposite*).

# INDEX

# THE GETAWAYS

## Vans and Life
in the Great Outdoors

This book was conceived, edited, and designed by gestalten.

Edited by Robert Klanten and Rosie Flanagan

Preface by Ruby Goss
Texts by Ruby Goss (pp. 5–8, 28–41, 54–109, 118–121, 142–145, 154–157, 182–185, 199–200, 218–231, 250–253, 265–275)
and Daisy Woodward (pp. 12–20, 46–49, 114–117, 122–139, 148–151, 161–175, 190–193, 205–213, 236–247, 258–261, 281–282)
Captions by Ruby Goss

Editorial Management by Anna Diekmann

Design and Layout by Carolina Amell
Layout Assistance by
Antonia Heckenbach and Joana Sobral
Cover by Melanie Ullrich

Photo Editor: Madeline Dudley-Yates
Illustrations by Livi Gosling

Typefaces: Quasimoda by Botio Nikoltchev
Bookmania by Mark Simonson
Superior Title by Jeremy Mickel

Cover image by Lukas Unterholzner / the-travely.com
Backcover image by Jonathan Steinhoff / @seppthebus

Printed by
Grafisches Centrum Cuno GmbH & Co. KG, Calbe (Saale)
Made in Germany

Published by gestalten, Berlin 2022
ISBN 978-3-96704-059-3

© Die Gestalten Verlag GmbH & Co. KG, Berlin 2022

All rights reserved. No part of this publication may be reproduced or transmitted in any form or by any means, electronic or mechanical, including photocopy or any storage and retrieval system, without permission in writing from the publisher.

Respect copyrights, encourage creativity!

For more information, and to order books, please visit www.gestalten.com

Bibliographic information published by the Deutsche Nationalbibliothek.
The Deutsche Nationalbibliothek lists this publication in the Deutsche Nationalbibliografie; detailed bibliographic data is available online at www.dnb.de

None of the content in this book was published in exchange for payment by commercial parties or designers; gestalten selected all included work based solely on its artistic merit.

This book was printed on paper certified according to the standards of the FSC®.